D1193286

Eros and Pathos

Marie-Louise von Franz, Honorary Patron

**Studies in Jungian Psychology
by Jungian Analysts**

Daryl Sharp, General Editor

EROS AND PATHOS

Shades of Love and Suffering

ALDO CAROTENUTO

**Translated by
Charles Nopar**

Originally published in Italian in 1987 by I Edizione Bompiani, Milan,
under the title *Eros e pathos: margini dell'amore e della sofferenza*

Canadian Cataloguing in Publication Data

Carotenuto, Aldo
  Eros and pathos

(Studies in Jungian psychology by Jungian analysts; 40)

Translation of: Eros e pathos

Includes bibliographical references and index.

ISBN 978-0-919123-39-7

1. Love—Psychological aspects.   2. Suffering—
Psychological aspects.   3. Individuation.   4. Jung, C.G.
(Carl Gustav), 1875-1961.   I. Title.   II. Series.

BF575.L8C37 1989   152.4   C89-095106-3

Copyright © 1989 by Aldo Carotenuto.
All rights reserved.

INNER CITY BOOKS
Box 1271, Station Q, Toronto, Canada M4T 2P4
Telephone (416) 927-0355

Honorary Patron: Marie-Louise von Franz.
Publisher and General Editor: Daryl Sharp.
Senior Editor: Victoria Cowan.

INNER CITY BOOKS was founded in 1980 to promote the
understanding and practical application of the work of C.G. Jung.

Cover: Paul Klee, *Love Song by the New Moon,* 1939,
watercolor on lined burlap (Klee Foundation, Bern, Switzerland).

Index by Daryl Sharp

Printed and bound in Canada by
Thistle Printing Limited

Contents

See final pages for descriptions of other Inner City Books

Acknowledgments

This book owes a great deal to my life and to those I have had the opportunity of knowing intimately. Some may see themselves mirrored here; others will feel the resonance of what we have known together.

I owe special thanks to Marco Balenci, Cristina Schillirò and Silvia Martufi for their helpful suggestions and proposals, and deep gratitude to my collaborators: Daniela Bucelli, Maria Fiorentino, Donatella Raspaolo and Anna Maria Sassone.

Introduction

Many years of analytic practice have made me familiar with life's two most overwhelming emotional experiences: love and suffering. Often we perceive them in ways that are distorted and disguised. It is as if we were all ashamed to admit that our souls are subject to burning with passion or breaking in anguish.

Even if it is not the primary reason, we go into analysis because there we can let ourselves go; it is there that we can vent our rage and our resentment against a life that often seems to bear the mark more of the devil than of God. In fact, to be fully human, to experience the whole spectrum of life, sometimes requires that we become deviant, at least from the standpoint of the collective.

Take love, for example, in the sense of a sentiment that binds two people who also desire each other sexually. Here is where models and guidelines inspired by general opinion are of no use. It can't be denied that the condition we assume to be normal—the love that lasts a lifetime, two partners who grow old together in continuing love— is in reality so rare as to practically constitute an anomaly.

The more "normal" relationships I have seen, the more I have come across hatred and sado-masochism. Too many unions are based on pathological need where each partner represents the other's sickness. The choice of a lover is based not on the "nice" parts of an individual but on the "worst" parts, those that belong to one's shadow. The lives of famous lovers—and it matters little if they are known to us from the chronicles of crime or from the pens of writers, they are all still part of the collective imagination—are fraught with terror and criminal acts.

Think of Macbeth and the fearful wife who inspired his crimes; think of Margarita who for love of Faust first kills her mother and then her child. Zola's Therese Raquin kills her husband with the help of her lover and thus realizes her desire to live with her beloved. But this ménage immediately becomes an inferno whose mute and paralyzed witness is the victim's mother. The story ends tragically: the two murderers confess their guilt to the old woman and then kill themselves before her eyes. These are lives consecrated to destruction in which there is not a breath of salvation. Their passion overwhelms them and like a demon takes possession of their minds and hearts. The love that unites them also indissolubly binds their shadow sides.

Such stories present a familiar sequence of events: falling in love, the decision to eliminate the obstacle, the complicity of the lovers in a murder, remorse, unhappiness, death. The malice that the force of love has brought to the surface explodes in all its violence; but the couple that lives through it cannot bear the consequences. Guilt and death enter, triggered by an inner law that is then externalized and puts the scales of the story back to zero. The death of the lover-killers presents itself like a necessary element to reestablish the order that has been subverted by the destructive force of love.

Love's transgressive power lowers the attention threshold of our conscience—with whom can we let ourselves go completely if not with the beloved?—creating a psychological arena where anything goes. In such cases, love liberates, frees us to express uninhibitedly not only our emotions but also our inclination to the negative, which in Jungian terms is an aspect of the shadow.

Think of Don Giovanni, perhaps the most famous seducer in Western culture, half historical figure, half artistic image. He is capable of perpetrating the most cruel acts on his those he enthralls, including leaving them. Don Giovanni lies shamelessly, betrays, abuses, kills. He is a man who draws energy from love relationships in order to leap the barriers of the moral code and fully live his shadow side. "Viva la libertà," Mozart's Giovanni exclaims at one point: what he is singing about is the liberty to do as much evil as he likes without feeling guilty.

This desire, present in all human beings, has great evocative power. Ruggero Raimondi, who played the title role in Joseph Losey's film, *Don Giovanni*, admitted to a journalist that he felt a great pleasure on the set in abandoning Donna Elvira. Don Giovanni, with the destructive force that is in him, is a paradigm of everything evil that can emerge from passionate love. In fact love, understood as an emotional storm that overrides the ego, exalts the criminal tendencies present in all of us. Even such a just man as King David of the Bible stains himself with blood when he falls in love with Bethsheba, sending her husband on an enterprise from which there is no hope of returning.

Love reveals us to ourselves. To paraphrase a famous remark of Joseph Conrad's—a man only knows himself in the moment of danger—we can say a person knows his or her true nature only through falling in love. Virtually every human being experiences passionate love at least once. And it is in this condition that our inner phantoms come to life.

If we investigate our behavior when in love we find not only tenderness, affection and emotional investment, but *always* negative elements as well. In order to understand the experience of love, its true importance, these dark aspects must be taken into consideration. For example, all lovers lie: sweet deceptions are the *leitmotiv* of love. This may seem incongruous, but deceit is by no means the worst we are capable of when consumed with passion. Love so activates the possibilities of self-knowledge that an entire universe heretofore unknown offers itself to the wide and curious eyes of the lover. The outside world takes on colors and shadings that are surprising while the inner world expands, receiving a spark of the infinite.

At this point an unbreachable gap is opened; as one's interior world becomes more intense and vibrant through love, the possibility of communicating one's perceptions becomes more remote. What emerges from our depths cannot be translated into everyday language. One is imprisoned by the inadequacy of words, and thus the lie, for instance, becomes a compromise between one's inexpressible inner reality and the desire to maintain the relationship. We fear the beloved will not be able to understand what we ourselves but dimly grasp. So we veil the truth, which, just because it is not reducible to words, can be frightening.

The underside of love, then, is a tangled web that weaves together such strategic threads as deceit, betrayal and jealousy. A precise yet fleeting force, hate, connects these. The conflict between love and hate is always present in passionate relationships even if it remains unconscious. This should come as no surprise, for wherever any emotion is present, so is its opposite. The interaction between these opposites may torment one, but it also constitutes the secret energy source of life.

For the most part, the destructive element lives in hiding within the sentimental bond, apparent only occasionally in a violent outburst that leaves the partners stunned and incredulous. But sometimes it emerges in all its force and even leads to murder, to what the newspapers call crimes of passion, committed for reasons of revenge, jealousy or despair. In literature and in the theater, as in life itself, love and hate are indissolubly linked. Even in his moment of homicidal madness the murderer may not stop loving his victim. Don José, after stabbing Carmen, says: "I myself have killed my *adored* Carmen." Thus the story of love is written in blood.

Yet love also inspires the noblest acts. Love actually demands the simultaneous presence of hatred. It balances within itself the poles of good and evil. That is what gives it a spark of the divine, briefly illuminating our pallid existence. Love can give meaning to an entire lifetime because it sets up resonances in the deepest abysses of our being. It is a lightning flash of the eternal within the flow of time.

But it is short-lived because no human can endure it. De Rougemont rightly speaks of love as a *myth*. In fact only in a mythical perspective can this sentiment find a psychic reality that is not bound by history and yet paradoxically influences it.

Love manifests itself in the world, yet it is not acceptable to the world. This can be illustrated by two films. *Elvira Madigan* is the story of female acrobat and a count who deserts from the army in order to run away with her. They are deeply in love, but soon encounter economic difficulties that lead to quarrels. The man cannot work because it would mean risking arrest as a deserter, but he doesn't want Elvira to sing for a living because he is terribly jealous. The inevitable happens: the count kills Elvira and then himself. This is not a film about love but about the impossibility of love.

The second film is Ingmar Bergman's *The Sign*. The story centers around a woman suffering from a grave mental disturbance and the man who is devoted to her. The woman has a speck in one eye and attributes to this all the sufferings of her life. When recovery in a psychiatric hospital becomes necessary, she blames the man and refuses to see him. After writing, "Love is the answer to everything," he deliberately wounds himself in the eye. Then he says to his wife, "Now I am the same as you; now I know how you feel." The film ends with their double suicide. Before dying they write a letter explaining the reason for their gesture: "We have come to realize that love is the only really important thing in life, but there is no place for love in this world and so we prefer to die."[1]

Death is the natural conclusion of love, not because that is what lovers want, but because the world cannot accept the subversive force of this emotion. Love breaks down the borders and subverts

---

[1] In this context, we can better understand the double concept of love-death, or *liebestod,* that enters Western culture in the twelfth century. According to De Rougement, it is the desire for annulment that lies behind *liebestod,* because only in extreme experiences do we come to know ourselves.

the constituted order so it *must* be annihilated. Laws cannot prohibit falling in love, but the collective cannot abide transgression. It leaves to die those who dare to bring a divine spark into the repetitious order of existence.

I do not mean this to be a condemnation of love but an invitation to reflect. We must become aware that though we thirst for love, we yet reject it because we fear it, and so take refuge in the flat banality of daily life. We must become conscious of this bitter and terrible truth: the world does not want love and it doesn't know it.

There are, of course, experiences other than love that permit us to penetrate more deeply into our psychology. One of these is mystic ecstasy, which involves the subjugation of the ego in a cosmic union with the divine. Another road to self-knowledge is the encounter with the gratuitousness of pain, whether physical or psychological. And there is the act of creation, in which we are obliged to plumb our depths. True, there is a fundamental difference between the pangs that accompany creative acts and the bitterness that pain instills. Yet both can enrich consciousness and encourage individuation.

There is also the helplessness we feel in the face of those who have power over us. At one time or another we have all felt excluded from the important events of the world, beaten down by those in authority The sense of exclusion grows within us, in the drama of our inner lives, fed by the insatiable desire for love that nothing and no one can ever satisfy. This manifests in the feeling of being poor when we have wealth, finding ourselves ugly when others call us beautiful, feeling disarmed and vulnerable when we are, on the contrary, strong (else we would not have survived). In such ways, by seeking an impossible ideal, we may end by failing to live, by slowly killing ourselves, day by day.

This book is about all these things: love and hate, pain, creativity, power, the need to balance outer life with the knowledge of our inner world. But mostly it is about the many dimensions of love.

No one, it seems, can convince us that courage and love can only come from within, that we are not given strength as a gift but must win it the hard way. The heroine of a novel by Erica Jong reads the fairy tale *Sleeping Beauty* to her little girl.[2] When the child asks, "What if the prince *doesn't* come?" her mother replies that the sleeping beauty will have to wake herself up and hug herself hard.

Only knowledge of oneself and self-acceptance can lead to independence, which in turn is the only basis for true relationship. And this also seems to be the only way to save our lives.

> Ah, love, let us be true
> To one another! for the world, which seems
> To lie before us like a land of dreams,
> So various, so beautiful, so new,
> Hath really neither joy, nor love, nor light,
> Nor certitude, nor peace, nor help for pain;
> And we are here as on a darkling plain
> Swept with confused alarms of struggle and flight,
> Where ignorant armies clash by night.
>
> —Matthew Arnold, "Dover Beach."

---

2 *Parachutes and Kisses* (New York: Signet, 1985), p. 150.

Come with me, I said, and no one knew
where, or how my pain throbbed,
no carnations or barcaroles for me,
only a wound that love had opened.

I said it again: *Come with me,* as if I were dying,
and no one saw the moon that bled in my mouth
or the blood that rose into the silence.
O Love, now we can forget the star that has such thorns!

That is why, when I heard your voice repeat
Come with me, it was as if you had let loose
the grief, the love, the fury of a cork-trapped\wine

that geysers flooding from deep in its vault:
in my mouth I felt the taste of fire again,
of blood and carnations, of rock and scald.

        —Pablo Neruda, Sonnet 7.

1
An Unexpected Occurrence

By its very nature love belongs to the realm of the inexpressible. Like everything that has to do with the soul, it is near to mystery and keeps company with silence. To leap the barrier, to give form to what cannot be said, is a wild, fearful enterprise risked only by artists and poets. Psychological investigation often stops short with a rational pseudo-understanding that violates the soul's reality. To raise the veil with which the soul covers its essence it is necessary to proceed with respect and trepidation.

To gather the thousand shadings with which we encounter the other, to venture into the labyrinthine world of images, means to abandon any single focus and give voice to all the daemons that live there. To write about love means to confront the inexplicable, to recount a subversive experience, give utterance to one's fantasies. However, since to read is to reinvent the text, to translate the author's imaginal world into one's own, the reader meets his or her own most intimate images.

A characteristic phenomenon of the love experience is that the presence of the other captures us with an intensity and an immediacy that is not to be encountered at any other time. The lover is bewitched and obsessed by the image of the other. This experience has an improvisatory, unreal and almost compulsive character. Plato went so far as to speak of a divine delirium, a kind of ecstatic rapture. In the presence of the beloved, one has a feeling of incredible fulfillment and at the same time the impression that until then one has lived in a state of deprivation. The presence of the beloved is truly a source of well-being and new life that seems to, nay does, have inexhaustible possibilities.

Proximity provokes this turmoil. We feel we have been captivated. But actually love is fed by what happens within ourselves. The one on whom my eyes and desire have focused takes on a unique significance for me and becomes irreplaceable, for only *that* person can invoke a deep and special inner dimension of my own.

Being in love always confronts us with the incomprehensible. The other person is *atopos*, that is to say unclassifiable, because definition implies knowledge of that other. For as long as love lasts, the attempt to stand face-to-face with the source of mystery and fascination really represents the attempt to translate it into a familiar and comprehensible experience. But even while we try to understand, to rip away the veil, we don't want entirely to abandon that illusion whose brilliance blinds us and so makes it possible for us to stay in love.

One remains in this condition for as long as the other is not to be grasped in his or her own spiritual dimension. Until that time something drives me to wonder about the values that just *that* face holds for me. Inasmuch as the beloved represents an inner significance, a significance of my own, the other becomes my only true interlocutor, the only one to whom questions can be put and an answer be expected—*the* answer, in fact.

The intensity and exclusiveness of the love relationship transform and enliven the way in which we interpret both external and internal reality. It is as if a multitude of images and emotions filled up our sensory channels, opening a new dimension to the soul. Anyone who has not been immersed in this experience at least once remains cut off from the world of the spirit and of the flesh. The beloved becomes a driving force toward the search for one's own truth, a window onto both the outer world and our own soul.

The love experience floods virtually every aspect of existence with the light of meaning. This can only happen when the other, whose image obsesses me, orients my psychic life incessantly in his or her direction. The power of this fascination is contained in the mysteriousness of the love-object, in its indefinability. The ability to keep the love experience going depends on the possibility of sharing with one's partner that inner enrichment released by the relationship.

Loving is an authentic psychological task, the most demanding there is, just because it activates in us new ways of knowing ourselves. The moment love enters the picture, you must learn to deal with an entirely new world. Everything is suddenly different. This change, which seems to be given to me by the other, has made a new person of me, and now my very way of seeing this experience, of living it, has been transformed.

When desire takes over, the body gets the upper hand. In our intense contemplation of the beloved—as if to discover the secret of that which binds and confuses us—we are looking for our past. The uneasiness excited by the other tells us how imperious is the need to reunite with something that seemed lost but now appears in a new and even more attractive light.

When we are inspired by desire, it is not only our voice that breaks, but all reality. External reality, previously so much in evidence, now takes second place. In its stead, as if on a revolving stage, there emerges a new universe, at the center of which are two lovers. From their point of view that universe is the only plausible one—but only from their point of view. For everyone else, the world of the lovers is an inexplicable abberation.

When we abandon ourselves to the power of Eros, all previous points of reference are impaired or swept away. Love makes lone wolves of us because we are less in tune with others and less able to communicate our experience. The only possible language is that of art or poetry. Its mysterious alchemical powers enable us to express what would otherwise remain forever hidden.

To become aware that others don't understand us is always a disquieting experience, but at the same time an exciting one because it makes us feel really unique. Further evidence of our uniqueness is given when we feel loved by the other, who is also unique, the only person who counts for us in that moment. Thus the uniqueness of the beloved crosses with our own. Such an encounter cannot help but create an exemplary, inimitable relationship. That is why, at the end of a relationship, we are perfectly justified in feeling let down. Something has truly been lost since no new encounter can ever bring that same experience back to life.

While it lasts, love is experienced as something definitive and perennial. When one has seen a love affair through to the end, one knows that love keeps company with the feeling of eternity. No one can love while thinking that this sentiment will come to an end. Anyone who wants to experience *psychic infinity*, that aspect of ourselves that transcends the limitations of physical existence, must enter the realm of love. At that moment we are disoriented, lose our bearings. But it is good that this is so. We must lose them. The fact of our being outside everyday reality, enclosed in what might be called a double narcissism, impels others to close ranks against us. We are lost to their lives, we have deserted, gone over to a different world. We are now strangers to them, incomprehensible and therefore frightening.

Another characteristic of love is that it alters our relationship with reality. The psychic order we have been used to is suddenly upset. We would not have been able to get ourselves into this kind of fix if our psychic structure did not allow for alterations. The upheaval of love is all it takes; apparently rigid attitudes melt away like snow in the sun.

In an old Arab love story as retold by the Persian poet Nezami, a young prince, Qeys (whose name comes from a word associated with the idea of measuredness), falls in love with the beautiful Leyla (night or darkness). When their love is hindered he becomes a prisoner of amorous delirium and wanders for years in the desert near the camp of his beloved until he dies. Thereafter he becomes known as Majnun, the love-crazed one.

As Romeo and Juliet symbolize the concept of love-death in the Western imagination, so Leyla and Majnun in the Eastern tradition represent the archetypal couple suffering from *amour fou,* passion that turns into madness. A madman is, in fact, one whose mind has clouded over. And Leyla, the love-object, in her double role as woman and night, wraps Majnun in her shadows. Leyla is compared to the moon whose light creates illusory forms. Love then is seen as a generator of images, of daemons, who with their explosive power alter or destroy all sense of proportion and balance.

We can always tell when someone is in love because people in that condition experience the object of their love as a source of infinite joy. And in fact they are not entirely wrong, for that particular moment is charged with a force no other can provide. But whenever we find ourselves going through an experience where someone else becomes the source of our ecstasy, we are certainly in an extreme situation. When I realize my happiness depends upon another person, I shake with fear. Having put myself in another's hands I am now at his or her mercy. It has often been said that success in life is dependent on our capacity for autonomy; but it is undeniable that the most profound knowledge comes from identifying in another the origin of our own joy.

Although completely abdicating our liberty can cause suffering just as intense as the joy we feel, we are in thrall to an emotion that cannot be avoided. Those who have been spared this condition are actually, in my experience, dead inside. Their armor is such that they feel nothing. For them life is eternally mute.

In the last analysis we are dealing with a phenomenon that disarms us in the face of life and imposes individual choices and decisions. As often happens also to a person beginning analysis, the lover is in the midst of an experience requiring a particular existential and psychological attitude. Paradoxically, one experiences a condition of renewal, even of rebirth, and at the same time the end of a part of the personality that was once vital to existence.

It is exactly the violent rupture of basic narcissistic defenses that characterizes the condition of love. One is jerked out of solitude and brought back into contact with unconscious aspects of oneself.

The condition of love makes one more disposed toward a new and wider psychic participation. But in order to be thrown back into the stream of life one must tolerate a sudden and uncontrolled loss of equilibrium, suffering a wound that puts into question one's entire existential order.

In the extremes of love and eroticism, we lose all certainty and become unbalanced. The ego begins to vacillate, to the point where we lose control of our behavior. This state of disequilibrium is a condition associated with being in love, but it is a necessary characteristic of any psychic transformation. It is also a state of mind we try to defend ourselves against. We instinctively sense the risk of being dragged into an experience that in all cultures is associated with the idea of death. All through history poets and artists have evoked death, the most fearful of specters, to give form and substance to this most intense state of attachment to the other. We cannot help trembling in such a situation because the erotic experience forces us to live through one of the most violent of inner conditions.

The vulnerability revealed by love and the central importance the other comes to assume in our lives throw us into a condition of need. Particularly during the first and most intense phase of falling in love, we are forced to live in a kind of solitude for two.

We are seduced by the other's way of being, of moving, by that glance, that voice. Certain characteristics of the loved one become irresistibly fascinating. They have, in fact, the gift of coinciding with our desire. This or that detail of the beloved, insignificant or even unpalatable in the eyes of others, becomes meaningful for me alone, who by loving discovers and succumbs to its charm.

As for beauty, it can be positively fatal in its effects because we are inclined to see in it a concrete correspondence to a highly interiorized need. But what exactly is beauty? The fact of having a body confronts everyone with an esthetic problem. People are sometimes cruel to each other, especially when they are very young. We have all known the burden of having a body that may or may not correspond to the esthetic canons of our culture. In reality we ought to become aware of the fact that beauty is a spiritual dimension, psychological, and doesn't concern only the object but also the way one perceives and relates to it. A form becomes beautiful because it is meaningful to an observer. This is because it coincides with an unconscious desire and thus succeeds in evoking it.

We can ask the origin of all this, how it is that an image becomes so important. Psychoanalysis has tried to answer this question by maintaining that the eyes that fascinate me with their mysterious mischief are those that gazed at me when I was very small, when I wasn't yet conscious of myself. This could possibly be the ontogeny, the remote cause for which a certain characteristic of the other acquires its significance. But with the passage of time this tie with the past no longer has much importance; what counts is that in a certain moment that gesture, that hair, that voice, those hands, can make me burn with desire. They are the beauty I seek; they are what coincides with the desire the other evokes in me.

This is the very essence of our experience—to find ourselves among a thousand people and become transfixed by a single image.

An inner dimension of mine of which I was ignorant has suddenly emerged and I am enriched by a psychic condition that was previously unknown to me. Thus, the image we call beautiful originates in our ability to create forms and give them life.

In the condition of love we are ravished not by the person we see before us but by the idea he or she has triggered in us, so that even at a distance we clearly perceive a particular face, voice, gestures and stance, all signs of our inner world that have been activated and brought to light by the encounter. As Goethe observes,

> Sometimes you are with a real person in the same way as you are with a portrait. He does not have to speak, or look at you, or concern himself with you at all: you see him and feel what he means to you, indeed he can even come to mean more to you, without his doing anything about it, without his realizing in any way that his relationship with you is merely that of a portrait.[1]

This powerful emergence of our inner images in response to the other, to the one and only other, explains why no one is replaceable in the love relationship. It is only this specific person who can activate this mechanism. It is enough to miss a telephone call or an appointment, or not be able to gets news of the beloved, and we are assailed by anguish. Describing such an experience, Barthes writes: "Waiting for a telephone call is thereby woven out of tiny unavowable interdictions *to infinity*: I forbid myself to leave the room, to go to the toilet, even to telephone. . . ."[2]

When expectations do not coincide with reality one is struck by panic, by a suffering that is almost physical. And in this precise moment—in the suffering provoked by the other's absence, in the violence of the desire that only the beloved manages to excite—the lover suddenly becomes aware of being alive. As Barthes writes:

---

[1] *Elective Affinities* (London: Penguin, 1986) p. 164.

[2] *A Lover's Discourse—Fragments* (London: Jonathan Cape, 1979), p. 38.

The deeper the wound at the body's center (at the "heart"), the more the subject becomes a subject: for the subject is *intimacy* ("The wound . . . is of a frightful intimacy"). Such is love's wound: a radical chasm (at the "roots" of being), which cannot be closed, and out of which the subject drains, constituting himself as a subject in this very draining.[3]

In inwardness we discover ourselves, we get to know our inner truths. The drama of this baptism by fire lies in the fact that it leaves a wound that never heals.

> I did the dragon's will until you came
> Because I had fancied love a casual
> Improvisation, or a settled game
> That followed if I let the kerchief fall:
> Those deeds were best that gave the minute wings
> And heavenly music if they gave it wit;
> And then you stood among the dragon-rings.
> I mocked, being crazy, but you mastered it
> And broke the chain and set my ankles free,
> Saint George or else a pagan Perseus;
> And now we stare astonished at the sea,
> And a miraculous strange bird shrieks at us.
>
> —W.B. Yeats, "Her Triumph."

---

[3] Ibid., p. 189.

He is more than a hero

He is a god in my eyes -
the man who is allowed
to sit beside you—he

who listens intimately
to the sweet murmur of
your voice, the enticing

laughter that makes my own
heart beat fast. If I meet
you suddenly, I can't

speak—my tongue is broken;
a thin flame runs under
my skin; seeing nothing,

hearing only my own ears
drumming, I drip with sweat;
trembling shakes my body

and I turn paler than
dry grass. At such times
death isn't far from me

   —Sappho.

2

The Evocation of Images

Love, in the sense of *concupiscentia*, is the dynamism that most infallibly brings the unconscious to light.
—C.G. Jung, "Transformation Symbolism in the Mass."

It is understandable that love was considered a disease in the Romantic tradition. We have already mentioned certain symptoms such as an altered perception of reality, the overestimation—to the point of the grotesque—of the value of the beloved, the need to limit drastically one's range of relationships. Thus it is not difficult to speak of a pathological state.

Stendhal expresses an interesting idea:

> Even little facial blemishes on other women, such as a smallpox scar, touch the heart of a man in love and inspire a deep reverie; imagine the effect when they are on his mistress's face. The fact is, that pockmark means a thousand things to him, mostly delightful and all extremely interesting. He is forcibly reminded of all these things by the sight of a scar, even on another woman's face. Thus *ugliness* even begins to be loved and given preference, because in this case it has become beauty.[1]

If this indeed be pathology, let us not forget that passionate love has traditionally been associated with artistic sensibility. To some extent, then, we are dealing with a most salubrious disease, one that awakens and strengthens creativity.

In truth, the enormous capacity Eros has to stir our imagination makes it an excellent divining rod for seeking out hidden veins of

---

[1] *Love* (London: Penguin, 1975), pp. 39-40.

25

creative energy. Naturally we are not speaking of formal artistic creation. The fact that love can rip a few couplets from the hearts of people who until that moment had never deigned to give poetry a glance is entirely irrelevant, especially in its results. We are speaking of that much more vast creativity that permits us to act autonomously in life.

A person in love feels unexpectedly capable of confronting even dangerous situations. For example, only someone in love can dispute the burden of the family: a youth who has never been able to say no to his parents is capable of burning the family furniture in order to pursue his projects when he becomes fascinated with his inner fantasy life. Unforeseen prospects open up and new possibilities emerge. Rilke says:

> Loving does not at first mean merging, surrendering, and uniting with another person (for what would a union be of two people who are unclarified, unfinished, and still incoherent), it is a high inducement for the individual to ripen, to become something in himself, to become world, to become world in himself for the sake of another person; it is great, demanding claim on him, something that chooses him and calls him to vast distances.[2]

When we refuse to love, when we do not consent to this encounter with the other, suggests Barthes, we are renouncing our fantasy life, this inner generating factor that only love can activate.[3] We might say that love is an unwelcome upheaval, but we must recognize that only from chaos can a new existence be born.

Though the remote etymological origins of a word may no longer have anything to do with its later meaning, it is interesting that the Latin root of the word "desire" *(de-sidera)* indicated the situation of a soothsayer who could not make his predictions because of the absence of stars (that is, because the sky was cloudy). It is also worth

---

[2] *Letters to a Young Poet* (New York: Vintage Books, 1986), p. 69.
[3] *A Lover's Discourse—Fragments* (London: Jonathan Cape, 1979), p. 87.

noting that navigators, since the beginning of time, have needed the stars to take their bearings.

Something of the same kind happens to a lover in the throes of desire. The external points of reference are gone. Love takes us off the beaten track, away from what we have long known; the realities we now encounter must be continually interpreted because they have no models in our past. Desire prevents us from understanding reality with well-known and habitual criteria. The most distinctive feature of such a situation is that it is always new, unfamiliar.

But the unknown generally inspires fear. That is why fear and being in love almost always go together, so much so that if in the midst of our excitement we do not also feel afraid, it is a good sign we are not really in love. "Love stirs fear," writes James Hillman. "We are afraid to love and afraid in love, magically propitiating, looking for signs, asking for protection and guidance."[4]

So we must ask then why we have this experience. Though it seems natural at the time, if one really thinks about it nothing is less natural than this feeling of living and being able to live only in the light shed by another person.

Probably this is a recent development and peculiar to the human race. Living constantly in a position of vital dependence, feeling mortally threatened by separation, or jealously demanding monogamy, are all well-known characteristics of the human lover. Even if one finds vaguely similar traits in a few animal species, we have developed the love dimension against nature, so to speak, without having an initial genetic provision for it. We have invented this way of feeling lacerated and of lacerating the other. Our experience is accompanied by fear because we have not yet mastered it. That is why it is so difficult to speak of this sentiment and why one must experience it in order to understand it.

---

[4] *Myth of Analysis* (Evanston, IL: Northwestern University Press, 1966), p. 81.

A sign of our true involvement in this rapture, then, is the accompanying fear that something destructive may happen. And this fear is justified because it is difficult to accept that the worst pains and sufferings that we inflict and are inflicted upon us mostly occur in the realm of love. Nor can it help but surprise us to discover that we inflict a mortal wound on the very person to whom we have dedicated our life and for whom we are willing to do anything. We can even commit murder.

> Passion means suffering, something undergone, the overbearing power of destiny on a free and responsible person. To love more than love's object, to love passion for its own sake, from the *amabam amare* of Augustine up to modern Romanticism, means to love and to seek out suffering. Love-passion: the desire for that which wounds and annihilates us is its victory. This is a secret which the West has never allowed to be revealed, continuing stubbornly to suffocate it.[5]

Anyone who loves is in a position to hurt the beloved, and, moreover, often does. This is not easy to explain. Perhaps the reason is that when we are in love we feel ravished and violated; and no one can conquer our inner self with impunity. So perhaps a person who feels totally possessed needs, however unconsciously, to take revenge by violating and hurting the other. We do not know. We only that love is full of fear; side-by-side with the most sublime emotions, it makes us tremble.

Love always brings with it a sense of mortal anguish, and tied to this is a feeling of ineradicable guilt. The depth psychologist explains this by the fact that we are dealing with feelings that are indissolubly linked, complementary but in dramatic conflict with each other: *prohibition* and *transgression*. The idea that love liberates is by now commonplace. But the facts are otherwise: to love and be loved means sooner or later to run head-on into the prohibitions imposed

---

[5] D. De Rougemont, *L'amore e l'Occidente* (Love and the West) (Milan: Rizzoli, 1977), p. 95.

by those around us. Our amorous enthusiasm is experienced by others as perilous and destabilizing. The metamorphosis that takes place in lovers calls into question the status quo. Society considers this an intolerable act of subversion and so vetoes it, obliging the lovers to become transgressors, to break those human laws which aim to conserve things as they are.

Whenever one rejects the experience of love by rationalizing it away, one is obeying a collective law that has been internalized. We have all absorbed this law that negates the free realization of desire in the face of life's continuous invitations. Thus, while life conspires to arouse us, it can—and does—often happen that we deny our desire in obedience to an external veto that by now is fatally alive within us without our even being conscious of it.

The misery, the impoverishment, the stasis that result are proportional to the strength of the impediment operating in us. I refer primarily to the dynamic process activated in the so-called falling-in-love phase that some may well consider only a first step subject to being normalized. But one should have the courage to admit that this initial phase could be permanent: this shattering experience rips me out of many sterile certainties and takes me beyond them.

In order to experience the full force of the tempest—which I myself have unconsciously sought—I must have the strength to neutralize that internal scream of menacing reproof. If we cannot accept the opportunity for growth we become sterile, greedy, dull, and the fantasy life from which we draw creative energy no longer vivifies. But it is crucial that our lives be illuminated by circumstances of this order. Past experience, the balance of all we have lived through, is only of limited help because, as Confucius said, it is like a light we carry on our backs and so it only illuminates the road traversed. Not only does it not light the road ahead, it does not even brighten the places we are passing through. If we don't turn on the light of our imagination we see nothing. Any experience, even the objectively richest, becomes the poorest in a subjective sense because it lacks the light of this fundamental dimension.

But why the veto? In common language the internalized veto is called the voice of conscience. Its function is to prevent anguish and forestall the terrible feeling of being hunted when we discover ourselves doing something for which we could be reproved. To keep from feeling guilty we respect the veto which in turn keeps the violence of desire at a distance. Yet desire is the very thing that gives us the strength to face life in a new way, puts us in contact with new values.

Let us see if we can clarify what happens when we talk of inventing the significance of the other. How often have we not said to someone, "You are so elusive," or, "I can't understand you," and how often has it not been said to us without our realizing that this is the very factor that initiates an evolutionary process. The first thing we feel on falling in love is the sense of an impediment: something or someone within tells us that we are hazarding onto a terrain that is not our own. By a strange coincidence, however, just as we sense the veto we also have the feeling—tenuous perhaps, but desperately tenacious—that we have the courage to break it.

De Rougemont queries:

> The obstacle . . . and the creation of the obstacle by the passion of the two heroes . . . is it only a pretext necessary for the development of the passion, or is it not rather connected to the passion in a much deeper way? Is it not, if you study the myth in all its depth, the very *object* of passion? . . . and yet the passion of love is, *ipso facto*, an unhappy state. For centuries the society in which we live (and at bottom its mores have not changed) has nine times out of ten dressed the passion of love in the garb of adultery . . . To affirm that love-passion is adultery *per se* is to insist that our cult of love works both to disguise and to transfigure at the same time; it is to put the spotlight on the dissimulations of this cult, on what it rejects and refuses to name in order to let us abandon ourselves to an ardor that we never dared lay claim to. . . . To judge by our literature adultery would appear to be one of the most remarkable activities to which

Westerners dedicate themselves: it wouldn't take long to write out a list of novels that make no allusions to it at all . . . without adultery what would be left of all our literature?[6]

The fact is that our psychological strength consists precisely in the capacity to fight whatever acts against our growth process. The moment we manage to perceive the obstacle and at the same time sense that we have the energy to neutralize it—that is the moment too in which the psyche becomes aware of itself. Hence whenever I do something that I "ought not" to, I leave the highway for a personal path. In choosing my own direction I become conscious of my existence. But just because I have taken on the responsibility of navigating on my own, awareness must necessarily be accompanied by apprehension and the fear of getting lost.

Nietzsche writes:

The general knowledge of mankind has been furthered to a greater extent by fear than by love; for fear endeavours to find out who the other is, what he can do, and what he wants: it would be dangerous and prejudicial to be deceived on this point.[7]

Plato long ago spoke of Eros as knowledge.[8] Love excites fear because what the other represents is something that requires continual interpretation. Paradoxically, of course, total interpretation would signify the end of this exuberant force that propels me toward the other. Love and fear go together precisely because they have the primitive quality of that which is unknown, because they involve elemental levels of experience that resist passing through the sieve of reason. They seize us, they dominate us.

It is my opinion that when this kind of fear is lacking, love is over or never existed at all. So I would say that the human being experi-

---

[6] Ibid., pp. 80, 60-61.

[7] "The Dawn of Day," in *The Complete Works* (London: T.N. Foulis, 1911), vol. 9, pp. 267-268.

[8] *The Symposium* (London: Penguin, 1951), 211c, p. 94.

ences the Self when he or she manages to be a transgressor. Bearing a prohibition and succeeding in getting beyond it is a risky business, but only then does one become aware of being human, only then is one truly alive.

It is a common experience that in solitude, when there is no outer stimulation to activate our fantasy life, we become aware of having a body. But it is as though it were foreign to us, as though it offered the opposition of an enormous inertia, as if each movement presented us with a bill down to the last penny for the fatigue it cost, and we were not able to pay it. Just so, when we lose the possibility of having our imagination activated we feel ourselves without strength. It is a sensation that is, or should be, more terrifying than that instilled by the adventure of interpreting the other with all its risks.

This danger is one reason why we resort to what Hillman calls magical propitiations: we consult the stars or a fortuneteller or the *I Ching,* all apotropaic rituals for containing the anguish caused by the relationship with the other. We become psychically inclined only when obliged to by the transgression and the anguish it causes us. And there is no reason to feel sorry for ourselves for having fallen so low, no reason to inveigh against our bitter destiny when love seems to present only its frustrating side. Phrases like, "I curse the day," or, "How many years have I lost on your account," are insults to truth: that day was undoubtedly a happy one, and those years, far from being lost, were the most profitable ones of our life.

As for the anguish, there is reason to suspect that it is an integral part of every vital human experience.

3
The Basis of Emptiness

There must be something magical in the experience of love if even people who generally avoid the irrational are overwhelmed by it. This return to an ancient fear surely has something to do with the fear of being dispossessed; but it is not unlikely that a more remote experience is also involved. Although it is legitimate to nurture doubts about so-called birth trauma, it is undeniably a separation. Our earliest experiences, though unremembered, leave an indelible mark on our inner world so that the drama of that original separation is a recurring theme from birth onward. It is quite possible, then, that falling in love fuels the illusion that a basic structural emptiness will be corrected.

Every relationship has its particular dignity. There is no such thing as an unworthy love or one to be ashamed of, because each experience corresponds to a profound individual need. And if and when it ends there is nothing to regret, because at that particular time the loved one filled our emptiness, no matter what happened next.

We are always inwardly driven to find what we lack. We can even reach the point of thinking that all external forms are hallucinations created by our imagination in its search for lost wholeness. If I am going through a period when I acutely feel this hunger, the other becomes a source of hope: the promise that I will become quite new.

It takes courage to live this experience without reservation because we have a rationalizing tendency that says, "I don't need anyone." This is a pitiful lie. Maturity has nothing at all do with the absence of desires. The emptiness that spurs us to search for an other to complete us represents a continuous promise of differentiation and change. Anyone who has had the good fortune to fall in love will attest to the metamorphosis that invariably takes place, even if the affair is short lived.

But the promise of wholeness always implies the risk of failure. My metamorphosis may be blocked and the other, after having represented my living hope, can come to be the witness of my failure to be transformed. This is most disturbing, because to have felt even for a moment that we could be different, to have imagined we could change, leaves us with a painful memory if we fail.

So we must learn to endure the privation. I think that to accept the emptiness is another structural feature of our existence. All our lives we struggle to seize something that eludes us, and in order to go on we must learn to carry the weight of the absence of the other. I believe that no therapy, no experience, can ever eliminate this sense of emptiness that love deludes us into thinking it can fill. When we feel the vacuum has been filled, we are deceiving ourselves. In fact, however well the beloved corresponds to our unconscious desire, the thirst for wholeness is so unlimited that nothing can ever completely satisfy it.

Our task, then, is to endure both the loss and the delusion represented by the beloved: whatever that person may represent or may have meant to me, he or she still stands for an absence. Indeed, we can say that each love affair dramatizes a myth: every time we find ourselves involved in such an experience we are reenacting the lost wholeness that goes back to our earliest moments.

Even more painful is our constant vulnerability to this feeling of emptiness. However much I may love another, and however much the other may requite my feelings, in every relationship there is the possibility of losing the beloved. And this fear is renewed more forcefully each time a new relationship is formed. But the loss takes us back to desire again. Thus, the fires of desire are ignited by the lack of something vital. In the case of love this lack installs the other forcefully in my inner world.

When the other is not present, we become obsessed by the *idea* of the loved one. If, on the other hand, the beloved is present, the characteristics we love become concentrated:

> Absent, your face expands so that it fills the universe. You reach the fluid state which is the one of ghosts. Present, your face condenses, you achieve the concentration of the heaviest metals, of iridium, of mercury. This weight kills me when it falls on my heart.[1]

Love, then, is intrinsically the experience of an absence, and absence is connected to nostalgia. It is as if throughout our lives we continually felt a deep dissatisfaction. We are moved by a sense of the infinite, whereas our achievements are always limited. If we look straight into the eyes of the person we love, even there we can perhaps read our reciprocal nostalgia.

We read in Plato that Eros's mother was called Penia, meaning poverty or need.[2] There is a static and a dynamic interpretation for this name: to feel deprived of something means to be spurred to search for it. In both life and love necessity drives us onward, but the search never ends, because whatever happens the result is always less than our expectations. Like Ulysses, humankind is forever embittered by experience, but dissatisfaction is the price we pay for growth. We know that personality only develops under the spur of what we are lacking.

Growth toward adulthood is also connected to the indomitable desire to obtain what we were denied as children. From a certain point of view, we are lucky this infantile state does not entirely disappear. It allows us, or better, forces us, to be different. The quality expressed in our readiness to accept new ideas and situations also enables us to make new discoveries. Whenever we cannot accept the absence of the other our imagination becomes activated: we begin to feel our human condition; we create completely new things whose

---

[1] Marguerite Yourcenar, *Fires* (London: Black Swan, 1985), p. 13.

[2] *The Symposium* (London: Penguin, 1951), 202b, p. 80.

existence we would never have suspected if we believed our needs were fulfilled.

There is no relationship that doesn't interfere with the feeling that we can grow, no love affair which is not burdened with resentment. Even as we feel an apparent fulfillment, we also realize that this is illusory. Something always disappoints our expectations and therefore we vaguely sense the loved one as an obstacle to real growth. Love that is given and love that is denied are equally painful and fertile sources of dissatisfaction.

Contrary to what is usually thought and written, it is not true that love is a fusion of body and soul, though this is precisely the illusion lovers try to realize concretely. Rather, the other continually evades our desire. At bottom, it is necessary to be alone, to taste one's own loneliness in order to understand what the presence of the other means. The fascination exercised by the beloved activates an interior dimension of our own and forces us to enter more deeply into our feelings. And the awareness of our aloneness is always deeply upsetting. In the last analysis love is the encounter between two solitudes because it is as if we always had before our eyes the image of ourselves desiring.

As soon as we come into the world we are obliged to experiment with preverbal contact. Immediately after birth one of the few instruments we have for understanding the world is our eyes, which normally meet those of others. This, in my opinion, is the origin of seduction by means of a glance. So it is that in their depth the eyes of the beloved connect us with the world. It is here that we once again encounter unsatisfied desire. Just as in earliest infancy the dialogue of the eyes was insufficient to satisfy our need to understand the world by way of the other, so in later life the electric meeting of eyes both enthralls and underlines the cosmic distance that separates us from the other. It is as if once again we were not able to experience anything more than our loneliness.

The moment I ask the other to represent on my behalf everything I cannot myself succeed in being, I feel again irremediable separation. I must make up for this loss and so I am perennially chasing after what I need in order to recuperate a lost wholeness. This search would in the best of cases be exhausting and painful, but it becomes real suffering when we imagine there is only one person in the world capable of completing us. How a conviction of this kind can arise is indeed a mystery, yet this is what gives such strength to lovers and is at the bottom of their complicity. It is as if they had really committed a crime. Only they understand what is happening, and however much good sense tells them they are going through an experience common to the whole human race, they feel it is unique.

One reason why the love experience always feels like something brand new lies in its remarkably complex and contradictory nature. Each time it happens, it is such an anomaly as to create the impression that it is in fact an exceptional case, outside the usual terms of reference. And yet it is just this contradictory aspect we must be able to accept and live through. Love takes on its shape and is legitimized to the degree that we are able to accept its irremediable ambivalence, its inherent contradictions.

> You are my slavery and my liberation
> You are my flesh that burns
> like the naked limbs of summer nights.
> You are my native land,
> you, with green lights in your eyes,
> you, tall and victorious.
> You are my yearning
> each time I know your elusiveness
> at the very moment I capture you.[3]

The beloved always symbolizes the potential of the lover. If I feel divided and I also feel the impulse to achieve wholeness, and if there

---

[3] Hikmet, *Poesie d'amore* (Milan: Mondadori, 1984), p. 44.

is only one person who personifies my potential, then that person actually becomes my hope, the incarnation of a possibility that only he or she can make actual. Thus we say, "I can't live without you."

From the moment the beloved enters my life, then, my whole previous history is called into question: I become aware that up to now I was not alive. In this sense the appearance of the other is truly an epiphany, for now I know that I will become something different, something I wasn't before.

It is evident that one enters the experience of transformation endopsychically. In the realm of love this phenomenon is more evident, I would say actually visible, just because an unconscious existential projection finds its living image in the other. Thus one is commonly said to be love sick, as if one had contracted a disease.

> My disease is different from all others; because I like it; it gives me joy; my disease is what I desire and my pain is my salvation. Therefore I do not see to whom I should complain about my disease; but I feel such pleasure in willing thus that I suffer pleasantly and I have such joy in my pain that I am ill among delights.[4]

And yet, the illness is nothing but a sweet promise that says, "You will be different if you unite with me." Such a promise is evidence for my present state of nonexistence, my being divided in myself.

The struggle between two lovers can also reflect the attempt of each to defend against the implications of this promise. Dependence causes resentment and hostility, reminding us of the danger of being needy. So we defend ourselves against our need for the other. This is a bitter experience. Not only does it makes our lives inauthentic, but worse, we block the possibility of transformation. Only by opening to the other, laying oneself on the line and accepting the acute reciprocal suffering of our dependence, can we find the vitality and strength to lead other than a banal existence.

---

[4] Chretien de Troyes, in D. De Rougemont, *L'amore e l'Occidente* (Love and the West), (Milan: Rizzoli, 1977), p. 82.

In a love affair, what fascinates is precisely the promise that the other represents. Though seduction is play-acting of a sort, there is no fraud, no bad faith, because by way of the other I most definitely bring my inner fantasies to life. They are authentic; they must be, for I am the first to believe in them and to involve myself in the game. And yet, the more intimate and habitual a relationship becomes, the more we become aware that the image which seduced us is in reality an interior image of our own.

> Tristan and Isolde do not love each other. . . . *Love is what they love, the fact of loving itself.* Tristan loves feeling himself loved much more than he loves the blonde Isolde. And Isolde does nothing to keep Tristan near her: she is content with a passionate dream. They need each other in order to burn, but not the other as he is in reality.[5]

Thus the greatest mistake we can make is to think that the other has seduced us. The truth is rather that I have been seduced by my own image. When I fall into the arms of my lover, ready for anything, in reality I am preparing to risk all for the sake of realizing my inner world. The lover offers the bait, is the instrument and the incentive, but it is something personal, something within me, that bites the hook.

Of course, it is never a question of pure and simple projection, though projections are inevitable. We cannot say that love is "nothing but" an illusion. The other exists—and how!—and must, for only the beloved, unique and irreplaceable, can evoke what I have it in me to be. Therefore statements such as, "You are mine," justifiably branded as uncivilized if taken literally as a claim to ownership, are psychologically true as tender expressions of a vital need one has of the other. Here the possessive adjective has no more—or less—weight than it has in the expression "my God."

---

[5] Ibid., p. 86.

This is the creature there has never been.
They never knew it, and yet, none the less,
they loved the way it moved, its suppleness,
its neck, its very gaze, mild and serene.

Not there, because they loved it, it behaved
as though it were. They always left some space.
And in that clear unpeopled space they saved
it lightly reared its head, with scarce a trace

of not being there. They fed it, not with corn,
but only with the possibility
of being. And that was able to confer

such strength, its brow put forth a horn. One horn.
Whitely it stole up to a maid,—to *be*
within the silver mirror and in her.

—Rainer Maria Rilke, *Sonnets to Orpheus.*

4

The Secret of Seduction

The main difference between a seduction and a relationship is that the latter does not demand total union but bases itself on the acceptance of separation and a realistic knowledge of the other.

Though we may long for total union, we know from experience it is a myth. To renounce that myth and detach oneself from the symbiotic fantasy it represents means that in a love relationship one will always feel separated from the object of desire. What I love will never be completely mine. Acceptance of this reality compels us to recognize our fundamental isolation even in those situations that seem to exorcise it.

Seduction, on the other hand, is based on an illusion. But it is an illusion that does have a *subjective* reality, incarnated in an image.

> I am as lovely as a dream in stone;
> My breast on which each finds his death in turn
> Inspires the poet with a love as lone
> As everlasting clay, and as taciturn.
>
> Swan-white of heart, a sphinx no mortal knows,
> My throne is in the heaven's azure deep;
> I hate all movement that disturbs my pose;
> I smile not ever, neither do I weep.
>
> Before my monumental attitudes,
> Taken from the proudest plastic arts,
> My poets pray in austere studious moods,
>
> For I, to fold enchantment round their hearts,
> Have pools of light where beauty flames and dies,
> The placid mirrors of my luminous eyes.[1]

[1] Baudelaire, "Beauty," in *Flowers of Evil* (Norfolk, CT: New Directions, 1962), p. 24.

In order to survive we must deceive ourselves about the things we do, about our love affairs, about our importance in the world. Where seduction is concerned we are invariably an object to the other person, whereas in what Martin Buber calls an I-Thou relationship, the other is rather a subject.[2] In an I-Thou relationship, two individuals meet and recognize each other as such. In the case of seduction, the subject becomes a phantom object.

And yet seduction plays a fundamental role in both transformation and self-knowledge. It compels us to work on appearances and at the same time to come to terms with our cognitive subjectivity. This means that through a seductive encounter I can get to know myself just as much as I can in an I-Thou relationship. The image I have of the other, an image that destroys or exalts my life, becomes an addiction. This image that seduces me will be the key—if I manage to grasp it—to understanding my personal behavior.

In a seduction situation the other becomes the light that turns on my world under the impulse of my needs. Behind the fascination lurks a hidden need and a personal, disquieting image. Just because we normally hold these at bay they acquire enormous power; at any moment they may become overwhelming and irresistible subversive forces.

To be seduced means to go off course, to be derailed. Remember that historically the devil has been the great seducer, causing enormous upheaval in human affairs. But it is precisely from this perspective, in conflict and crisis situations, that we have the possibility of becoming authentic. Seduction thus involves a psychological state that allows us to understand aspects of ourselves that would otherwise remain unknown. When does this experience occur? Whenever we deserve it. Blessed are those who manage to be seduced, for they will know themselves much better. The relationship with these hid-

---

2 See *I and Thou* (New York: Charles Scribner's Sons, 1958), and Mario Jacoby, *The Analytic Encounter* (Toronto: Inner City Books, 1984), chap. 4.

den parts, these dark elements—aspects of what Jung called the shadow—becomes the prime focus when we are seduced.

The seductive agent is a kind of drug that gets into our system and will not go away unless we let it run its course and succeed in metabolizing it. Here we encounter aspects of ourselves we are ashamed of and so keep in darkness. Only when our back is to the wall and there is no hope of defending ourselves does the Self emerge to show us the way out. The person who seduces us has become an agent for knowledge and truth.

Indeed, not even sex can take place between humans except by way of seduction. In itself the sexual element is meaningless without seduction, because even in this case one must create a subjective image of the other. And this, incidentally, is a piece of great good luck because in this way we can choose an "ideal" partner who, in terms of an outlet for sexuality, becomes potentially very significant for oneself though not necessarily for others.

Seduction calls into question every attempt at a scientific discourse on sexuality, because generally we tend to attribute our sentimental moods to the tightly-knit play of biological signals and responses. But this is to ignore a factor that in humans has become more important than anything organic: the imagination.

One might go so far as to say that deceit is essential for our souls. We must be able to deceive ourselves because only by passing through error can we move toward our personal truth. If we have not continually dreamed throughout our experience of love, our reality as creatures who subjectively take a stance facing the other will not be able to emerge, because we will mistake something else for the real and the true, something that does not correspond at all. The only area in which we can authentically recognize ourselves is our psychic individuality, and this creates the reality of love.

> What I have written about is all lies
> it is my yearning

grown on the unreachable branch
it is my thirst
drawn up from the well of my dreams
it is an image
traced on a ray of sunlight
what I have written about us is all true
it is your grace
brimming fruit basket spilled on the grass
it is your absence
when I become the last light at the farthest street corner
it is my jealousy
when I run by night through the trains blindfolded
it is my happiness
sunlit river flooding the dykes
what I have written about us is all lies
what I have written about us is all true.[3]

The poet's privilege and gift is to accept the contradictions in both outer and inner life. As for those of us who have chosen to investigate the psychic life, contradiction is a constant and ineradicable fact. The psychologist is constantly running into ambivalence, which is to say the contradictory nature of sentiments. Statements such as, "I want to and I don't want to," "I love you and I hate you," "I am attracted and repelled," are the only ones that can express correctly much of our emotional life.

Seduction is really and truly a revenge of the psyche over the body, over appearances. Only a superficial spirit can believe that one can dominate another by means of forms, of shapes, and take possession in the most brutal and savage sense of the word. In reality, there is no level on which lust can hold the line against the psychic impressions that, though evoked by the presence of the beloved, yet manage to inspire true affection.

Seduction is the weapon of choice in relationship. From the moment of birth, the infant with round face and huge eyes sets off a se-

---

[3] Hikmet, *Poesie d'amore* (Milan: Mondadori, 1984), p. 101.

ductive process that inspires tender feelings in the parent. This first imprinting conditions and informs all our future relationships. Every time we meet another person, for whatever reason, we perform the rite of seduction, though it may take place in absolute silence. One's aim is to conquer by exciting in the other a psychological factor of which that person is unaware. As we do this to others, so it is done to us. Seduction upsets reality because we are not conscious of being seduced.

Life can be read as a continuous upheaval of knowledge and equilibrium in the attempt to gather meaning. During the gradual process of growth we must at some point lose our identity as individuals: we lose ourselves in life, in outer reality. But much of what we find outside is self-constructed. When I am ready to risk my entire life to possess someone—even to the point of committing the most vile actions—I certainly forsake objective reality, but I gain a new understanding of myself. Those who go through this experience abolish the world's truth and substitute an hallucinatory image; and they seldom realize that those emotionally overwhelming forms that appear to come from outside are precisely their own.

We are impelled to seek meaning in our lives. Generally we look for it outside ourselves, but the one true explanation is received only when we become aware that what has seduced us is the image we carry within. For this reason too it makes no sense to attack and point an accusing finger at the seducer. True, the seduction may be aided and abetted by a deceitful masking of the other's true character—those who boast of being great seducers are generally people who *allow* projections to be made upon them—but it is my own unconsciousness that prompts me, as in a mirage, to glimpse in the other an image that hooks me.

In cases of seduction, the spirit seems to be captured precisely by the lack of definition in the other. This is never absolute and objective but always relative and subjective. No one, of course, is an empty shell but what may be lacking are the contents and meanings we are impelled to attribute to the other. This might lead one to think that we are condemned, forever anchored to a certain type of internal image. But it can also be seen as a possibility of experiencing ourselves in diverse ways throughout our lives, for the internal images are always changing. In other words, inasmuch as I am the one who invests my experience with a certain meaning, each moment in time can be enriched with different meanings.

How many people, when looking back and trying to find a thread that links their emotional involvements, recognize that the images each time were similar? This is why seduction is inevitable. No one can avoid it. What really creates the irresistible interest is the question posed by the other to the subject. And it is the subject, myself, who must bear the burden of it. Thus seduction involves an interrogative: I ask myself tormenting questions because the other, *ipso facto*, cannot be entirely "solved," entirely understood, but remains *terra incognita*, an inexhaustible adventure. As do I.

> I knew it was you. Seeing the print
> of your foot on the path,
> I felt the pain of your trampling in my heart.
> I ran madly; I searched all day,
> like a dog with no master.
> You were gone already! And your foot trampled
> my heart, in a flight without end,
> as if that were the road
> that took you away forever.[4]

In truth, the dilemma posed by the seducer really becomes the most important question in life. When my clinical work brings me into contact with people suffering in this way, I see how the problem raised becomes an obsession, to the point that it also has physical consequences. Sometimes the physical suffering can only be elimi-

---

[4] Jimenez, *Poesie d'amore* (Rome: Newton Compton, 1983), p. 47.

nated by the presence of the person who has activated those questions. Every request, which can also take on strong regressive tones, asks, finally, for the pain to be alleviated. The seducer has pressed a button that has never been touched before. In that moment there are no ready answers, though one readily deludes oneself that the seducer can provide them.

There are obvious aspects to a seduction that partly explain the fascination of the seducer; but there is always a hidden aspect too. It is a dark experience capable of weaving a spell that is impossible to explain to anyone else. And when we are ingenuous enough to try, we discover we are truly faced with the ineffable. We can describe specific characteristics, but that serves no purpose because seduction itself, our obsession, cannot be described, it can only be lived.

Observe two people in this situation. We notice that the seducer never speaks but expresses his or her presence by implication, while the one in thrall pursues the other and tries to find satisfaction in whatever can be understood through intuition. The beloved is seductive because he or she leaves us guessing—speaking cryptically or not at all—leaving us to interpret how we will. But in reality we only understand the other to the extent that he or she is already part of us. Seduction locks us up in a labyrinth and forces us to confront the Minotaur who has lured us into it.

The challenge is to fight and kill the Minotaur. That is legitimate self-defense. Seduction draws us into a duel, a duel that can even, or only, be fought with glances. The eyes exert a great fascination because through looks we can love and hold secret discourse with the other, leaving no traces. The eyes, windows on our soul, speak with an eloquence denied to words, probably because the language of the eyes was the very first language we learned. Looks help us to understand words better.

The voice also exerts an immediate fascination. Perhaps its attraction too goes back to infancy and the mother's voice. One always speaks to new-borns in a specific, reassuring tone. We remember the voice and some of its particular qualities as we look into the eyes of those who love us.

> Your voice! I heard it first,
> pure, like that windblown
> font in the freshness
> of morning.
> Your voice! I hear it now
> in the golden setting
> of my living dream,
> star in the last light
> of the sun.
> Your voice! Peace of m
> awakening to a new day; sweet
> blue nocturne for my rest . . .
> Your voice![5]

Voice, a glance, aroma, a certain carriage, that so-seductive gesture—everything that concerns the other, all the hidden meanings, are the source of seductiveness. Like love, seduction lives on secrecy, on the constant need to discover the evasive sense of something hidden, something between presence and absence. This something that we seek in the other is at the roots of our being. There is no introspection, no other experience, equal to love for putting us into contact with the unconscious. Only through love can we really get to know ourselves. But it is also painful, because in the end we will have to acknowledge that the secret of the other is actually the result of psychic projection.

At bottom, many psychological sufferings are connected to the difficulty, if not the actual incapacity, of allowing oneself to be seduced. To be seduced means to lose one's certainties. Thus, if we are impervious to seduction we remain in a state of childish innocence, not having ever had the opportunity of really knowing ourselves.

---

[5] Ibid., p. 49.

The most beautiful pages in Jung, as in the writing of anyone who succeeds in expressing his or her creativity, derive from a seduction experience that coincides with becoming conscious of one's own interior world. This is a painful road, one that can lead to madness, but who would choose innocence, even sanity, over enchantment?

> A damsel with a dulcimer
> In a vision I once saw:
> It was an Abyssinian maid,
> And on her dulcimer she played,
> Singing of Mount Abora.
> Could I revive within me
> Her symphony and song,
> To such a deep delight 'twould win me,
> That with music loud and long,
> I would build that dome in air,
> That sunny dome! those caves of ice!
> And all who heard should see them there,
> And all should cry, Beware! Beware!
> His flashing eyes, his floating hair!
> Weave a circle round him thrice,
> And close your eyes with holy dread,
> For he on honey-dew hath fed,
> And drunk the milk of Paradise.

—Samuel Taylor Coleridge, from *Kubla Khan.*

When your face
appeared over my crumpled life
at first I understood
only the poverty of what I have.
Then its particular light
on woods, on rivers, by the sea,
became my beginning in the coloured world
in which I had not yet had my beginning.
I am so frightened, I am so frightened,
of the unexpected sunrise finishing,
of revelations
and tears and the excitement finishing.
I don't fight it, my love is this fear,
I nourish it who can nourish nothing,
love's slipshod watchman.
Fear hems me in.
I am conscious that these minutes are short
and that the colours in my eyes will vanish
when your face sets.

—Yevtushenko, *Colours.*

5

The Sacredness of the Body

There is an aspect of love that is much talked about: the *making use* of another human being. The lover invariably feels like an object with which the beloved may take liberties. This is a voluntary loss of subjectivity. In addition, by desiring another, one also reduces the other to an object. A person in love constantly experiences this basic contradiction, this dynamic conflict triggered by the desire to be both a subject and an object.

The body becomes the symbol of this conflict. There is a moment in life when we realize we are made of flesh. Some say we feel this most deeply through pain, but we also discover the body by means of desire, which not only objectifies us but also reveals our corporality. Thus we can understand what it means psychologically for someone to discover that he or she is no longer loved: it is as if one had suddenly become invisible.

When those eyes no longer desire me, those hands no longer trace and caress my physical shape, my body is "dimmed," does not exist. Previously the other valued my presence and showed it, confirming my physical boundaries. With the waning of interest my lover shows no awareness of my body. That is a kind of death.

In being loved and desired we become flesh in the hands of someone else. And so whoever loves me makes possible the miracle of my incarnation. Obviously we exist physically from the moment we are conceived, but we only really take possession of our bodies when we meet someone who desires us. As soon as we become aware that someone lusts after us, we learn something; consequently it is a cognitive moment. From then on one has a new and extremely important way of apprehending oneself. When we are desired, our sense of self no longer coincides with our personality but with our carnal existence, and this transformation is due to desire.[1]

This experience also has great dangers, which explains why people are so afraid of becoming objects of lust: when that happens we abandon our subjectivity, our existence as individuals is threatened. But it is just this loss of subjectivity that makes room for new experience. At this point we are taken over by the illusory process that marks a love affair. For it is the individuality of the beloved, the subjectivity that includes all of that person's unique experience, that we are trying to capture by body contact, by penetrating the flesh, smelling the odor, seizing the hair, all with pleasure.

To enter this world and make it our own is the most exquisite conquest one can ever make. The illusion consists in thinking that we can really conquer another's subjectivity by objectifying him or her as flesh, *as* a body. It is an illusion because body contact, however overwhelming and emotionally charged, can never unveil the mystery of the other's essence. This is a contradiction from which no one can escape. We have all been driven to test the possibility of knowing another by experiencing him or her as object, neglecting the other's psychic life. There is a deep psychological reason for this. To be turned into an object shows that one can share a life with someone separate from oneself; it means we have the capacity to personify another's desire.[2] All the subtle nuances of a relationship say the same thing: you and I objectify each other .

---

[1] When in the course of analysis we meet a person who neglects him or herself physically, the prognosis is often pessimistic because it means no one desires that person. One who is sexually desired is never neglected. It is not a question of beauty in the usual sense, but the awareness that grows within when we feel loved. Then we realize our individual beauty; without a relationship one cannot arrive at such knowledge.

[2] Very often I ask myself, in the first sessions with a new analysand, "Has this person ever been embraced?" There are cases where one has the impression that except by the mother, this person has never been held, objectified, and so has missed the opportunity for self-knowledge through another.

The experience of body contact is even deeper and more necessary than nourishment. Touching and caressing represent basic and essential ways of knowing and loving. By caressing I mold the other's body, follow and discover its contours, giving shape to the flesh; I regenerate it and am regenerated. Naturally there is the attempt to find the beloved out, to discover his or her secret through this contact. The most significant aspect of a relationship lies in just this inexhaustible possibility of being, whose deepest levels can hardly be tapped. There are people who have known each other for many years and who still manage to experience the erotic encounter as a novelty because the hidden element they seek is never revealed. When there is no more mystery, indifference takes its place.

Erotic relationships are extremely important because feelings of security and physical well-being are greatly enhanced by our being loved. The feeling of affection received is internalized precisely on the basis of our earliest experiences of body contact. This inevitably contributes to our self-confidence. Love makes life intense and meaningful. Thus, when we perceive great change in another, it is less likely due to intellectual growth than to a love experience that has given a new shape to his or her life.

Faith in one's physical existence and faith in the psyche cannot be separated; one is the mirror of the other. It is natural, therefore, to experience a profound kind of communication via the flesh. Physical proximity is the most direct and intense form of nonverbal communication. It is renewed in the moment of danger or fear or tenderness, akin to the time when the mother pressed her child to her breast. Such moments are reevoked and relived in adult life and grant us the possibility of communicating silently.

Nonetheless, the renewed sense of one's body can be a source of fear. When we love passionately we are more tied to life, but also more aware of death. The body of someone in love is always naked —however clothed—simpler and more exposed, with the fragility of every creature that goes back to being more intimately itself. The ideal situation for really understanding another is not so much how a person reacts to extreme stress, but rather how he or she suffers the vulnerability of falling in love.

In a love affair we are defenseless before the beloved. The sense of nakedness is due to the exposure of the most jealously guarded areas of our inner world. To make this visible induces shame because it is tantamount to a confession of weakness. There are some people who, though they love intensely, do not show their feelings because they are afraid of the consequences. The lover feels that something has been lost, something that touches deeper aspects of oneself. A vital part of oneself has been sacrificed, exactly as one makes an offering to a god. In this case the body we donate is to be understood as a part of our psychological life. We feel trapped, tied up in a situation from which there seems no release.

And yet, despite the weakness and state of neediness that love imposes upon us, the poet can write:

> Oh blessèd be the day, the month, the year,
> the season and the time, the hour, the instant,
> the gracious countryside, the place where I
> was struck by those two lovely eyes that bound me;
>
> and blessèd be the first sweet agony
> I felt when I found myself bound to Love,
> the bow and all the arrows that have pierced me,
> the wounds that reach the bottom of my heart.
>
> And blessèd be all of the poetry
> I scattered, calling out my lady's name,
> and all the sights, and tears, and the desire;
>
> blessèd be all the paper upon which
> I earn her fame, and every thought of mine,
> only of her, and shared with no one else.[3]

---

[3] Petrarch, *Reflections from the Canzoniere and Other Works* (London: Oxford University Press, 1985), p. 35.

Petrarch thanks and blesses everything, but many a lover feels differently. Full of fear and screwing up our courage, we declare our love at the risk of being rejected. In order to reveal our feelings, we have to imagine the other waiting to receive us with open arms. It is this fantasy that gives us courage. At certain times we must be able to live on illusions and fantasies, in order to find the strength to expose ourselves and ignore what might happen in our confrontation with reality. The natural flow of energy is blocked if we entertain the specter of defeat. And in general, when we strip ourselves naked it is the fear of rejection that arouses our anxiety.

To reveal oneself means, in the end, to concede part of one's freedom and I would almost say parts of oneself, physical as well as psychological. Love is, in fact, an extreme case, a borderline case, where the physical and the psychological meet and mingle. That being in love can be so painful, with repercussions on the physical level, is proven by the fact that when the loved one is absent the suffering this causes can make one ill. Poets know this, and we can give their real meaning back to verbal commonplaces by forcing ourselves to understand the physical implications of such words along with their metaphorical meaning. As Barthes affirms:

> Endlessly I sustain the discourse of the beloved's absence; actually a preposterous situation: the other is absent as referent, present as allocutory. This singular distortion generates a kind of insupportable present; I am wedged between two tenses . . . : you have gone (which I lament), you are here (since I am addressing you). Whereupon I know what the present, that difficult tense, is: a pure portion of anxiety.[4]

To give ourselves to the person we love means both to abdicate our autonomy and to imagine it can only be returned to us by the person to whom it is given. This is the vicious circle of love seen from the standpoint of declaring oneself: I can manage to offer myself,

---

[4] *A Lover's Discourse—Fragments* (London: Jonathan Cape, 1979), p. 15.

open my heart to the other, only at the risk of my independence—which only my beloved can give back to me.

To declare one's love has diverse implications, but its deepest and most fundamental value lies in understanding that when you say to someone, "I love you," you are actually affirming yourself, in that you show yourself capable of stripping yourself bare and accepting the consequences. It makes us vulnerable because declaring oneself involves the most secret and shameful emotions. Hell and heaven meet at this time as at no other. From this moment on, and for an indeterminate period, our lives will seem to have stability only if it is possible to recuperate that which has been "stolen."

Having the courage to reveal one's inner feelings is in fact a sign of maturity; it means one is able to risk oneself. It is a common experience to have recklessly revealed oneself to no avail. Thus it is natural to ask ourselves if it is courageous or foolhardy to repeat the experience. I would answer that it is always important to take the risk, because even if our love is not returned, aspects of ourselves that were hitherto unknown become visible. When things go well and we get as good as we give, a type of harmony is created that covers up the wrong notes in our personality. When, however, we meet with rejection, we are repaid with psychological knowledge, which, however painful, can be especially rewarding. We can say, "I was capable of displaying my vulnerability, of making my request; I was able to give life and breath to those psychological entreaties that the beloved evoked in me and challenged me to express."

Making this psychological state evident is a crucial moment in our lives because it is then that our fantasies come alive. Undeclared, loving in silence, we forge our love object, give it shape, construct a world of possibilities. We create a condition that is not perilous as long as it remains imaginary. As soon as I expose myself, however, I implicitly accept the possibility that my imaginary universe can become real, incarnate in the beloved. This is truly frightening, because what I see is my own image. Let it be said yet again—the person I love is not really as he or she appears to me because the beloved is charged with my fantasies and my constructions. Having revealed myself, I see my gift hovering before me like a ghost.

How often have we fantasized a relationship, how many times have we invented marvelous appearances to adorn a situation, and how often, luckily, did these come true! These are moments of absolute rapture, because it is not often that we get to touch our inner images in the flesh. And we do know that we are dealing here with fantasies we have created ourselves, because when there is no longer any reason for these to personify themselves in that person, the beloved means nothing to us.

Thus, the beloved also represents the danger that our personal experience may be made futile. Whether or not the fantasy is real has not the least importance if my partner can create a different inner world with me. When this hand shapes a body, it is implicitly the work of one's own inner world. Thus, the more creative capacity we have, the more we are able to confer depth on those near to us. Moreover, the bitterness we can feel in remaining with someone who no longer gives us anything can also be an accusation against ourselves—for not being able to draw on our imagination to invest the other with the ability to personify our inner desires.

To show love means to accept everything, the prospect of joy and suffering, fullness and desolation. The mistake into which we unfortunately fall is to think that we must at all cost exclude conflict and suffering. This is utopian, because if we ourselves are bearers of an inner split, and we ourselves bestow life and death, there is no union where this dichotomy will not emerge.

Enormous suffering is an intrinsic possibility of every bond; we cannot refuse a relationship because it might bring pain. To reveal one's feelings is to say yes to oneself. Our ingenuousness deludes us into believing we have found a path that excludes this fracture, but in reality, when we have said yes to someone, we have said yes to both life and death.

When I accept the challenge of confronting the coexistence of life and death I am forced to measure myself not so much with conflictuality as generally understood, but with my personal conflicts. Therefore the courage or the fear of opening one's heart expresses the courage or fear of knowing oneself intimately. To reveal the love one feels means that my desire takes on reality and each declaration—each "I love you"—becomes a repeated affirmation that does not regard only the beginning, but also the continued existence and possible end of the relationship. Every moment of staying together is a reciprocal confirmation.

We are dealing here both with an act of love and a continual request for it. In the circularity of a love relationship, my fantasies are personified in the one I love. I have succeeded in exciting in my beloved a world unknown to both of us; that becomes the site of our continuous revealing of ourselves.

There is of course a reward for all this. When we reveal ourselves, we implicitly recognize that our own inner world personified in the other, our fantasies and expectations, are unique to us and must be accepted in order for them to be brought to life. That is why we must expose ourselves, why we must reveal our fragile world of affects to one who may deny its realization. It is worth the trouble.

6
Suffering for the Other

The most intense pain a person can suffer is that derived from the sphere of passion. There is no human condition comparable to love for making one accept the burden of suffering for another. This may seem strange to those who suppose that love must unfailingly bring happiness, but that is an illusion we create for ourselves in order to survive the interminable hours of suffering. Only those we love can make us suffer with the same intensity as we love.

The pain of love deeply involves the whole person, like an open wound. The psychological sensation of union, in the beginning even more of identification, with the other makes the beloved the center of one's life, almost a part of oneself. Therefore the lover is inexpressibly vulnerable to any absence or deficiency in the beloved.

Even if the other remains by our side all our lives, the sense of his or her presence will vary, because the emotional tie is a fluctuating one, full of contradictions. This generates pain because absence can be experienced as the loss of a vital part of our own being. In the condition of love, at least in the first phases, our physical constitution changes; in union with the beloved our metal is transformed, we create a new alloy. This fusion, however, can be lost at any moment, and we are seized by anguish.

Think of the beginning of a relationship: it is all fantasizing. When we tell the person who interests us those three words, "I love you," we are doing nothing more than laying the foundation for telling the beloved our imaginings about him or her. This fantasy of love is our invention, because so far we have not known the effective reality of the other. This is crucial to an understanding of the phenomenology of this moment: the lover has fantasized about the beloved, has day-

59

dreamed, has invented an entire story, but when the love is declared, that is no more than affirmation of the lover's own inner life. Having reached this point, the lover is asking for the chance to animate his or her fantasies and desires, to transpose into language and relationship the emotion that has been activated.

This involves a fundamental change—the clash with reality, the getting down to hard facts. It is a critical moment because the projection has the chance of becoming a reality in which the lover's own condition is joined by a new element.

From this point of view the encounter can be compared with an initiation. What love gives us is hope for psychological totality because it was our psychological lacunae that created the conditions for it. In reality it is an initiation that never ends, because the lacunae will never be entirely filled. But when we have tasted the extraordinary sensation of fulfillment that being with the other gives, we will always have at least the knowledge of where our emptiness lies. The first experiences are fundamental, because they provide the imprinting that continually allows us to recognize outside of ourselves the cause of our sense of incompleteness.

The dramatic but also highly stimulating aspect of this process of initiation is the one I referred to before: once begun it never ends. The risk in this feeling of totality is that it is dynamic and not static. As we grow psychologically, we are constantly changing, so it can happen that we lose the beloved because we have reached the point where he or she no longer fills our sense of emptiness. This is the drama we constantly face in the course of our love experiences.

And this too is why some people think that to declare oneself is a reaching out for conquest: if the other represents something I lack, I must seize this treasure, steal it from the world. Just when we succeed in capturing that which gives us a feeling of completeness, we also feel, with terror and anguish, the possibility of losing it.

There may well be relationships that have no light and shadow, no shivers and presentiments, but they are associations of another kind. Love is characterized by the alternation of separation and reunion, by the incessant need to reaffirm possession, to say, "You are mine forever," while at the same time a secret voice whispers, "Surely that is not so." To partner someone for good is not a one-time thing but a continual achievement.

Absence evokes solitude and not just a single solitude. The fact is that the moment we discover the feeling of being entirely at one with the beloved, we also perceive our isolation. The feeling of emptiness is what allows us to understand solitude as an opening, a desperate opening, to the other. This permits us to perform certain gestures which are also acts of courage.

The experience of union goes hand-in-hand with that of separation. It is as if an existential condition condemned us to this inescapable knowledge: to find also means to lose. Wherever this duality is missing, where there is apparent security, there is seldom a vital relationship. The deeper the tie, the more necessary we are to each other, and therefore the more we fear loss. In this deep union, we who lean toward the beloved also recognize his or her fundamental difference. We may know it is an illusion to believe our feeling of totality is guaranteed by the presence of the other, but it is too enticing to do without. There is no psychological process that can fill up this necessary illusion in which is implicit the recognition of distance and diversity.

A true psychological relationship must include recognition of difference and distance. On the other hand it is precisely the psychic distance that allows the pair to stay together, because one experiences the presence of the other, who, however, is absent by virtue of being different. One finds oneself back again in the initial solitude, but now with a big difference—it is an isolation that has put up a struggle and has managed to open itself up. The strength has been found to look at how things really stand,. To see reality means to have a deep understanding without dissolving the tie, because that would surely be an infantile response.

Strength consists in accepting this diversity. It is not an accident, it is neither good luck nor bad, it is the necessity implicit in that particular phase of life that confronts us with a need which must be experienced to the hilt. In precisely these moments we get support from the thought that our encounter always has a dynamic balance: its history and its depth reflect our level of maturity. The encounter is continually being recreated, therefore it can be transformed as our needs change.

Though there is bound to be conflict when the projections of two lovers meet, at no other time is there so much reciprocal influence. In this condition, where two people change, each in the other's direction, we feel we are pervaded by something new and something old: the new thing is the transformation underway and the old is nothing other than the rediscovered subjectivity in the relationship—that which created the love and gave it its poetry.

7

Self-knowledge and Eroticism

The encounter between lovers is characterized by the return of a more ample subjectivity. At the beginning, in the falling-in-love phase, the lover's individuality is confused with that of the beloved. But when the relationship really begins we are returned, transformed, to our separate selves. This is where we come to recognize ourselves anew in the bond we have created. Thus every love encounter is like an artistic creation. What fascinates and gives depth is the fact that nothing can be taken for granted, there are no formulas. Both partners are responsible for the dimensions, form and development of the relationship.

But here we come to the question of personal commitment. Within ourselves we bear a desire, absolutely healthy, to create a relationship after our own shape and image. Within the possibility for constructing something, one understands that the other ought to be considered a continuous discovery. If one is courageous, one confronts unknown lands and tongues and encounters things never before imagined. In the beginning one suspects nothing, because, like oneself, the other has a mysterious private essence. The beloved has a reality as legitimate as my own, one which my desire must come to terms with.

Life's greatest vicissitudes take place in just this area—the difficulty of taking into consideration the uniqueness of the other. Some speak of destiny, but it is we ourselves who create the situation that allows for an encounter requiring justice and room to move. It is interesting to find that our subjectivity is particularly underscored by factors that arise in precisely this relationship between two individualities. Our authentic essence emerges with all its lights and shadows. That is why there can be no psychological growth without the meeting and clash of two worlds; from this encounter emerges both my uniqueness and that of the other.

One cannot approach the dark side of one's personality except by comparison with another person. Therefore whenever one simply passes from one superficial relationship to another, evading the deep encounter, this can usually be understood psychologically as a difficulty in one's relationship with oneself. Indeed, in refusing to give in to love, we deprive ourselves of a golden opportunity for self-knowledge. Only if we accept our emotional life as it is can we understand ourselves. Our unworthiness and perversity only emerge in the intimate encounter with another.

Jung maintains that in the analytic relationship the highest and lowest aspects of human spirituality come to the fore.[1] The same may be said of a love relationship. When our ferociousness emerges and we find out how violent we can be, we also learn where our strength and our inspiration lie, because if we are able to do one thing we are able to do its opposite too. I can only see my light and my strength by peering through my darkness.

The moment one accepts the premise of such an encounter—be it analysis or love—there arises the possibility of creating a new essence, a new condition that can only spring from the relationship. We can call it an illusion or projection, we can say it is false, but what counts is our feeling that synthesis is only possible with that specific person. Subjectively, a surrogate for the other is unthinkable. In such situations we say things like, "You will never be able to forget me"—and it is true, because once this essence has been pro-

---

[1] "The Psychology of the Transference," *The Practice of Psychotherapy,* CW 16. [CW—*The Collected Works of C.G. Jung* (Bollingen Series XX), 20 vols., trans. R.F.C. Hull, ed. H. Read, M. Fordham, G. Adler, Wm. McGuire (Princeton: Princeton University Press, 1953-1979).]

duced, even for a short time, the circumstances that brought it about become unforgettable.

It is understandable that we tend to make the love experience eternal, and although the feeling of eternity is subjective it also has its deep truth. However, experience tells us that the encounter degenerates when I rediscover my individuality; at that moment the element of power comes into the picture. It only takes a minor shift in feeling for the one who seems indispensable to the other to be strongly tempted to use this as a weapon. And so the situation may slowly change from a healthy exchange between two subjects into a damnable conflict.

A relationship offers us space and time, and the time is always the present. It is not possible to imagine a tie between two people that does not include this particular dimension, where the uniqueness of each is discovered and realized. According to Martin Buber, love is the very space of the relationship.[2] When one loves one relates to a Thou who is understood and recognized as the exclusive subject of the relationship. I remove the other from the inanimate world of things, from the condition of being an object for me—as happens in every power relationship—and I restore to my beloved his or her dignity, integrity and power.

The exploitation of another is a real and true perversion, and yet one must realize that in any relationship, along with the possibility of having a Thou with whom to dialogue, one always runs the risk of losing oneself, of becoming an It. A good image of this comes from Buber, that of the chrysalis and the butterfly. The chrysalis is a form in a nascent state, a creature that should develop and reach its perfect condition by becoming that which it potentially already is. The chrysalis is formative life whereas the butterfly is manifest subjectivity.

---

[2] *I and Thou* (New York: Charles Scribner's Sons, 1958), p. 30.

Just because a relationship calls upon the specific character of each of the partners, the difficulty can—and generally does—consist in recognizing and accepting one's individuality as it emerges in comparison with that of the other.

In a love encounter each person moves toward the other because he or she activates a new and indispensable psychological factor that is experienced as lying outside oneself, personified in the other. Eros creates the ties between the various psychological elements, conferring meaning, inwardness and sacredness on the erotic experience. If a human being becomes important by activating the divine in me, I must always keep in mind the fact that my subjectivity is bound to a new and sacred dimension. And here two important elements enter into play that one could call light and shadow.

To create the particular essence that is bound to the singular characteristics of two people, I must go through a reading of my perverse sides. When the shadow emerges, it is as if there had been a catharsis in me and I had given birth to something entirely new that had some sacred and mysterious quality. Because of this sacredness, we get the feeling of being entirely alone, of not being able to impart our experience to anyone.

In this context is born the intensity of our sexuality, and also our individuality. Because sexuality has long been subject to prohibitory limits, it is in this area that our approach to another person becomes particularly dramatic. We may believe ourselves to be unconstrained, but this shows itself to be a delusion whenever we are seriously presented with an opportunity to freely express our sensuality. Therefore we could say that the art of loving, of eroticism, coincides with transgression. By way of the erotic, human beings are enabled to break the internal prohibitions—to veto the veto.

One can in fact develop and acquire a fully human character by way of the erotic. When we approach the other erotically, we are no longer spectators of nature but rather subjects of the pleasures we experience. Our imagination aids and abets in breaking the veto. Our capacity for transgression is directly relevant to the development of the erotic. By breaking the taboos we understand that the senses can only express themselves when they live within the orbit of prohibition, that they feed on what is prohibited.

But human sexuality is never, like that of animals, completely instinctive, because the imagination always plays a part. The consciousness of having a sexual experience inspires fear, anguish and guilt, and the ability to enjoy one's instinctive life free of these feelings requires great psychological maturity. Few are spared negative experiences of sex between infancy and adolescence. There are two aspects to this: on the one hand there is my desire which makes me feel guilty because deep down I feel I am doing something I should not, and on the other there is a sense of transcendence, the possibility of sublimating or transforming my desire so it becomes spiritual (as with the mystics).

Desire has disturbing connotations, for when I desire another person I am really aspiring to possess his or her animal aspect. One could say that this kind of experience leads us into an extreme situation that unhinges our habitual way of relating to the world. With our senses we overstep a limit, becoming aware that the cultural order to which we hitherto subscribed can be abolished.

An erotic encounter constantly impels us onward because the limits tend to recede. A deep sexual emotion can only be experienced by way of a lengthy relationship, the only kind that allows time for the cultural limits to expand. And it is precisely this receding of the limits that triggers our anxiety, for it feeds on those internal vetoes we are wont to call inhibitions.

How my body blooms from every vein
more fragrantly, since you appeared to me;
look, I walk slimmer now and straighter,
and all you do is wait—who are you then?

Look: I feel how I'm moving away,
how I'm shedding my old life, leaf by leaf.
Only your smile spreads like sheer stars
over you and, soon now, over me.

Whatever shines through my childhood years
still nameless and gleaming like water,
I will name after you at the altar,
which is blazing brightly from your hair
and braided gently with your breasts.

—Rainer Maria Rilke, *Sacrifice.*

8

Fear of Loss and Jealousy

Inhibition clashes with compulsion: one paralyzes, the other drives us forward. That is why the sexual attraction between two people may endure. But these two forces create a sacred space which is the secret site of every love affair. Thus we can understand why lovers might object to the beloved's relationship with another.

We must understand these feelings and realize that to some extent they are justified, inasmuch as the involvement of a third person violates the hallowed ground established between two people. Of course, these things happen because we are old hands at profaning, but the indignation and repulsion we feel have their roots in the sacredness of the relationship.

In the area described by inhibition and compulsion dwells a mystery which is the very basis of good and evil. Just when the erotic bond becomes predominant, and one has the feeling of having created a sacred dimension, we experience the impossibility of being able to recreate that space elsewhere. By joining together we could present ourselves for rebirth in the world, but when there is a crisis in the relationship our whole existence is impaired. Fearing the end of everything, we yet notice, far off but steady, the distant promise of a possible rebirth.

Compulsion drives us to the edge of an extreme condition, one that could be described as the desire to incorporate and to be incorporated. And it is here that the archetype of the mother appears.

> A burning tripod bids you be aware,
> The deep of deeps at last awaits you there,
> And by that glow shall you behold the Mothers.
> Some of them seated, some erect, while others

69

May chance to roam: Formation, Transformation,
Eternal Mind's eternal recreation.
Around them float all forms of entity;
You they see not, for wraiths are all they see.
Pluck up your heart, for peril here is great .[1]

The desire to incorporate and to be incorporated manifests itself in that most tender expression of love, the kiss. Just as the child seeks life at the mother's breast, so the adult seeks it from the soft lips of another. When we no longer feel the desire to kiss the other, the relationship is in danger. I have heard people say, "I can go to bed with him (or her), but I cannot kiss someone I don't love." This is an indication that sexuality is not tied to specific organs, but is diffused. The mouth, which is our first way of getting to know the world, of taking and receiving love and life, later becomes a gauge of the most profound sentiment.

Here we find ourselves entangled in a fundamental dichotomy that in reality expresses our brutality: the violence of death and the very hardness of life which are at the bottom of our capacity for erotic response. In the presence of the reflections on life and death which can emerge from a love affair, the first thing to be impaired is our subjectivity, but it is just through losing it that we can experience the sense of union. This is an illusion because one can never completely possess the subjectivity of the other. And thus it is that sexuality is destined to repetition. Without a certain psychological understanding of ourselves, the sexual instinct becomes inhuman, a desperate effort to grasp the other. Such sexuality is far from the expression of a great love. And yet the repetitive sexual impulse is also part of our destiny and becomes a ritual.

Of all the animals, only humans can love and desire constantly and unceasingly, unbound by the cycle of mating seasons. But for a

---

[1] Goethe, *Faust* (London: Penguin, 1986), part 2, p. 557.

healthy relationship desire must be mediated by another aspect of love—tenderness. How often have we not noticed moments when the vehemence typical of sexual desire took second place to it.

Tenderness works in opposition to the great threat that comes from the sense of death and loss. One could say that our deepest feelings of violence and tenderness are connected by the never-ending fear of losing the other. That is why we need to confront each other, through words and gestures—to confirm in some way our presence. We might even say that eroticism derives at bottom from the desire to live in uncertainty. It is as if the deepest spring, that which impels us to keep life going by procreation, were not the desire for happiness but for anxiety. No wonder, then, that the loss of the beloved becomes the simulacrum of every relationship. Some accept the challenge and some cannot.

When the fear of losing one's beloved totally invades the psyche we can properly speak of anguish. This is the terrain which germinates an emotion tremendously difficult for us to confess to, but one to which it is still harder to remain immune: jealousy.

Jealousy is a feeling immutably tied to love: lovers cannot help but know it. When we discover we are jealous, we suffer from anxiety. This intense and dramatic reaction is a concrete reenactment of our experience in the primary relationship with the mother. From this point of view the jealous reaction is functional.

An emotion that notoriously blurs our vision of external reality and darkens our inner landscape nevertheless turns out to be illuminating with regard to knowledge of ourselves, for it tells us what we expect here and now from the other: an exclusive love, unlimited and single-minded affection. Thus jealousy recreates and gives immediate force to a vital need of the child.

It is unnecessary to explain why the need for love is vital in small children. In the early phases of life we grow and develop only through the love of others; without it, we are permanently wounded. So then, if our growth, above all our psychological growth, is bound to this need, the fear that accompanies the possibility of losing the beloved is a signal that we are in danger. We often say, "I cannot give you up." Our suspicion and possessiveness result from our belief that our life has a future only because the other exists. That is why the doubt is so devastating.

We can say it is simply the fear of losing support from the one we love. But if we really face our jealousy, we realize that it calls up a whole series of psychological devices that have to do with aggression. "Jealousy," writes Proust, "is often only an anxious need to be tyrannical applied to matters of love."[2] Having arranged things in such a way that I am obliged to be jealous—for it is never by accident that one chooses the kind of relationship in which this emotion is bound to emerge—I have created the conditions for an unconscious tyranny.

Suspicion, bedfellow of jealousy, justifies everything. There is no act we are incapable of committing under its impulse. Suspicion of our mate brings out our shadow in full force. The unconscious drive to possess another person propels us into relationships where it is inevitable that we will express our jealousy, behind which is the shadowy desire to tyrannize. To our everlasting chagrin, it becomes a proof of our insecurity.

Where a sentimental bond is concerned every gesture assumes a wider meaning: a kiss, a caress, a word, everything is magnified by our psychic investment in the other. Thus it is not sexual infidelity per se that causes anxiety in the jealous person but rather the fear of losing what the erotic element represents in the relationship. The moment there is a deviation in the attentions of the loved one, we

---

[2] *Remembrance of Things Past* (New York, Vintage Books, 1982), vol. 3, p. 86.

sense a betrayal of everything. That is when we are confronted by our inner child, terrified of losing love and support. It is the fear of abandonment.

Paradoxically, infantile factors such as jealousy and possessiveness are in reality the basis for personal development. Anyone who is not jealous is not authentic, hence we must preserve our capacity for being jealous. It is true that jealousy can also express merely the desire to be at the center of attention, and in general its highly intense and unrealistic manifestations are symptomatic of psychological problems. But it is also true that we only become truly aware of love when this experience is intersected by the dramatic and irrational phenomenon of possessiveness. It is as if we had to experience love as anxiety, as the desire to live in uncertainty. Mlle. de Lespinasse expresses this dramatic aspect of being in love: "I love you as one must love, in despair."[3]

Perversely, we maintain and renew our suffering by constantly bearing in mind the possible loss of the other. At times it seems as if one only felt alive when loving in this way. On the other hand, the person who craves power cannot live in this state, which is why power and love cannot coexist. A person consumed by the will to power cannot be head-over-heels in love because this implies, among other things, being completely absorbed by something that can be lost at any moment—and being powerless to prevent it.

Jealousy is the source of such suffering because the one who is prey to this feeling has arrived at the conclusion that without the beloved life has no meaning. This brings the lover face-to-face with his or her sense of incompleteness, knowledge so full of anguish that just the specter of it keeps us from letting ourselves go. To face this experience, as I've said, takes courage.

---

[3] R. Barthes, *A Lover's Discourse—Fragments* (London: Jonathan Cape, 1979), p. 48.

Jealousy is a humbling experience. Anyone who has never let go completely, never accepted love with all its risks, including possessiveness, has lived an inauthentic, we could even say inflated, life. A sign of maturity is the acceptance of one's pettiness and neediness. To admit the possibility of being jealous means assuming the risk that one's life will evolve only on condition that the beloved person is by one's side. Of course this is infantile, but the child within will have its say and we must be prepared to listen.

Barthes writes:

> As a jealous man, I suffer four times over: because I am jealous, because I blame myself for being so, because I fear that my jealousy will wound the other, because I allow myself to be subject to a banality: I suffer from being excluded, from being aggressive, from being crazy, and from being common.[4]

We must allow for the possibility of feeling jealous and we must permit ourselves to experience it to the hilt. And this means to make the shadow conscious. It is wrong to think that jealousy can be overcome through will power.

Jealousy is meaningful because it allows us to begin a new kind of confrontation. The true declaration of intent between two lovers takes place within the range of this emotion. Before it arises we live in the illusion of eternity. When we become aware of our jealousy, we are forced to reevaluate the relationship and so another phase begins, one in which the two lovers meet again on new ground.

The realization that the other might *choose* to leave throws everything into question. Relationships must be constantly reviewed in this light. Moreover, when we are in love we tend to deify the other and this makes the situation more dramatic. We are possessed by our blind faith in the other. Of course no human being can tolerate

---

[4] Ibid., p. 146.

for long being deified, and it is jealousy which provides the road to a more realistic view.

In the final analysis, the destruction of a faith which we have constructed ourselves allows a veil to fall away: now we can see clearly that the loss was not a remote possibility but an ever-present and current reality, an unavoidable element of the love affair. Again, Barthes says as much:

> It is the fear of mourning which has already occurred, at the very origin of love, from the moment when I was first "ravished." Someone would have to be able to tell me: "Don't be anxious any more—you've already lost him/her."[5]

Since I lost you, I am silence-haunted;
  Sounds wave their little wings
A moment, then in weariness settle
  On the flood that soundless swings.

Whether the people in the street
  Like pattering ripples go by,
Or whether the theatre sighs and sighs
  With a loud, hoarse sigh:

Or the wind shakes a revel of light
  Over the dead-black river,
Or last night's echoing
  Makes the daybreak shiver:

I feel the silence waiting
  To sip them all up again,
In its last completeness drinking
  Down the noise of men.

        —D.H. Lawrence.

---

5 Ibid., p. 30.

The old man has the earth by day, and by night
he has a woman that's his own—that was his own till yesterday.
It pleased him to uncover her, like opening the earth,
to contemplate her at length, recumbent in the shadows
waiting. The woman smiled with her eyes closed.

The old man tonight is seated at the border
of his open field, but he doesn't scan the streak
of the distant hedge, he doesn't reach with his hand
to uproot a weed. He contemplates between the furrows
a searing thought. The earth reveals
whether someone has laid hands on it and violated it:
reveals it even in darkness. But there is no woman alive
who retains the marks of a man's grasp.

The old man has realized that the woman smiles
only with her eyes closed, waiting supine,
and understands suddenly that on the young body
the clasp of another memory passes in a dream.
The old man no longer sees the field in the darkness.
He has thrown himself to his knees, clutching the earth
as if it were a woman and could speak.
But the woman stretched out in the dark doesn't speak.

Where she is stretched out, eyes closed, the woman doesn't speak
or smile, tonight, from her mouth bent
towards the bruised shoulder. She reveals on her body
finally the clasp of a man: the only one
that could mark her, and it has extinguished her smile.

—Cesare Pavese, "You, Wind of March.

9

Betrayal and Abandonment

Rivers of ink have flown on the subject of jealousy; the bulk of all theater pieces, fiction and cinema deal with it dramatically or grotesquely, tragically or comically. But the interesting question is not what possessiveness can lead to but where it comes from.

A psychological approach always takes us back to an inner condition describing the endopsychic reality that lies behind a specific situation. In the realm of jealousy we are in a highly agitated situation since it is not only a torment that overwhelms and flattens our lives but also has a propulsive and cognitive effect. The triangle seems to be fundamental to the love experience, to such a degree that even in the rare cases where this third element does not intervene in reality we invent one on the level of fantasy.[1]

This need for a third person is rooted in the Oedipal triangle we have all experienced since birth. Father and mother reappear in our lives when, as adults, we relive that which we witnessed in the past. This threesome is frequently recreated secretively in an adulterous liaison, and in certain circumstances is acted out in a *ménage à trois.* Such experiences, which generally are related to the psychologist with great anguish or guilt, do not need to be evaluated moralistically; they can be read and understood in terms of the need to relive the Oedipal situation.

Possessiveness confronts us with our shadow side and that is why it is worth experiencing. Jealousy suggests the loss of the primary object, the first love of our lives in whom we put absolute faith.

---

[1] See James Hillman, "Psychological Creativity," in *The Myth of Analysis* (Evanston, IL: Northwestern University Press, 1966), p. 97.

Desperately, in every emotional tie, we want to recreate that faith which in the course of our infancy was shattered. At times we are so anxiety-ridden by this need for complete faith that we are impelled to fantasize about being abandoned by those we love.

We may feel a vague need to be liberated from this impossible faith that has marked our existence, but we seldom give a form to this desire. Perhaps if we were to succeed in putting it into focus, we would realize we were on the wrong track, because it is not thus that we will become adults. Rather we must find the strength to accept and experience completely the most absolute abandonment, especially by the prime object of our love.

The loss we fear in a relationship has in fact already occurred. We no longer have a father and a mother to protect us, and if we nourish any such hope it is but an illusion—so fervent an illusion that it even succeeds in creating in the outer world parental images that perpetuate the existence of our real mother and father. When one understands that one has already lost all, then one begins to take up the cudgel with oneself. Even in the case of genuine betrayal I have the chance again to understand that it is not my beloved who is betraying me; it is not he or she I must deal with, but myself as both betrayed and betrayer.

Just because we have had that initial experience of being abandoned, we bear within the possibility of becoming adults. Yet alongside that possibility there remains the hungry desire of childhood. Luckily, we are capable of reigniting desire—we can resurrect the dream of recovering the original love object and the early trust we lost. Every time we establish a relationship in which to relive this primary emotion, we lay the foundation of a house with an open door for betrayal to enter in and settle down.

The experience of deceit—which includes both the betrayer and the betrayed—signifies the anguish of loss. It lays down its roots and flourishes, making the other important and meaningful. Personal qualities have nothing to do with it. If we do not understand that, we are at the mercy of the first comer.

At the moment of betrayal a wound is opened in our most vulnerable spot—our original trust—which is that of a totally defenseless infant who cannot survive in the world except in someone's arms. This is the primitive and basic reality of the child; it is embedded in the psyche to the point where we can never dominate it. Inevitably, then, this helpless child reemerges in any relationship where there exists the possibility of putting unlimited trust in another person.

Poetry illuminates the subject of betrayal and abandonment. It depicts human existence as a devastated landscape; it goes beyond the world of appearances and puts us into hard and cruel contact with things we blindly refuse to recognize. Obviously the person who abandons or deceives us is not an evil person who hatched this plan in secret. He or she is only a human being to whom the gods offered the chance to live a new love experience. It cannot be relinquished because in that moment it becomes as indispensable as a primary need. But to we who are betrayed this truth matters little; we know only the terrible hardness of fate, pain for which there are no words, a devastation that grips the spirit.

We can only be deceived by those we trust. Yet we have to believe. A person who won't have faith and refuses to love for fear of betrayal will certainly be exempt from these torments, but who knows from how much else he or she will be exempt?

In general, we would like to be protected from our temptation to not live up to our commitments. We don't want to betray or be betrayed because betrayal forces us to confront the less controlled aspects of ourselves. And we hold them off even by trying to avoid love. This is because love is experienced also and inevitably in an infantile manner, with all an infant's verve, immaturity and inadequacy. There is the tendency to surrender to an illusion of a regained original trust which will then necessarily end by clashing with the hard reality of deceit.

Betrayal must be seen in perspective. We must not set ourselves up as judges and make a wholesale condemnation of the other, who then, like Lucifer, is cast out of the role of angel and into that of devil. In this way we deny anything good and lovable we ever saw in that person. They have not essentially changed; only fate has taken them away. If I were to be asked how to become an adult, I would reply that the road leads through such experiences, because in them we face again our primal loss.

I remember a letter Jung wrote to Sabina Spielrein where he says that it is not in him to love except for love's own sake, without any other motive, without the need of justifying his behavior, without the need of promising anything.[2] These are words to sign one's name to without hesitation. What sense is there in loving only when you can have total confidence? This is an infantile demand.

Think of Judas. Leaving aside the letter of the Evangelists, no writer who later took up the problem of Judas ever doubted his love for Jesus. Despite the fact that his name very quickly became synonymous with traitor, it is not possible to give anything but an ambivalent meaning to the expression, "kiss of Judas." If he had not loved Christ, his act would not appear so treacherous. Furthermore, his betrayal was a necessary step, a *felix culpa,*[3] in the story of the savior's ransoming of mankind. Judas was the indispensable instrument that set off one of the greatest revolutions in history.

Traitors risk destroying their inner world if they cannot integrate their ambivalence. Their drama is that they cannot carry through a

---

[2] See Aldo Carotenuto, *A Secret Symmetry: Sabina Spielrein between Jung and Freud* (New York: Pantheon Books, 1983), pp. 195-196.
[3] Fortunate crime.

single relationship to the end. By having two lovers, for instance, one can drastically reduce one's commitment to a relationship that one would not be able to bear in its totality. The consciousness of this helps to avoid an otherwise shattering sense of guilt.

When one feels the need to deceive the beloved, this implies a lack of integration of the shadow. On the other hand, the person who betrays can be considered faithful to life, for the unconscious aim of betrayal is often to transform the initial tie: "I do not have the courage or the strength to change the existing relationship and so, with the violent impact of a third person I will revolutionize it and see what happens." It is as if deceit were the only instrument left with which to break down boundaries.

This usually happens unconsciously. There may be external motivations, but they are superficial. I am convinced there is always complicity, albeit unconscious, between betrayer and betrayed. There is no need to investigate; one always knows what the other is doing, one just doesn't talk about it. One can even see in betrayal an attempt to preserve the relationship. In reality the betrayer is also the victim of the person deceived, who, in turn, becomes a traitor. Already at this point, of course, there is a crisis, with one of two possible results—a fruitful restructuring of the relationship or, more commonly, a search for new life: in other words, abandonment.

The experience of betrayal, translated into psychological terms, provides the opportunity to experience one of the fundamental processes of psychic life, the integration of ambivalence, including the love-hate feelings that exist in every relationship. It must be emphasized again that this experience does not involve only the one who usually takes the blame, but also the betrayed, who unconsciously set in motion the events that led to betrayal.

What does the end of a relationship mean? Above all, it means the collapse of a psychological order. In moving close to a psychology different from our own, we have structured ourselves differently. The relationship modifies us, because the need to unite with another and maintain a relationship sets off transforming mechanisms that allow for harmony with the beloved. With rupture and abandonment, this set-up is overturned and fundamental aspects of our existence are called into question.

In relationship we no longer base our lives on our individual selves, our own resources, but on the continued presence of another. Though the rupture can lead to a new situation with a new balance, first there's the fall.

What can one do in these desperate moments? There are no models for the broken-hearted lover. The end of each affair has its own special identity with no points of reference in the external world. No words can reach us, no change of scene console; the overwhelming despair seals us off and precludes the help of others. Reason and reassurance are ineffective because we are flooded with memories of other moments, now lost, that gave us our identity.

Here again great courage is needed. We encounter this loss every time as if it were the first. Loss and abandonment imprison us in solitude. No experience is as tragic because there is no external resource—and I would say not even an internal one—that can help us. Our only recourse is to work through our isolation. One was alone in the realm of love; one is even more alone now, in tortured silence. This suffering is a revelation; we know it will never end, just as shortly before we knew love was eternal. Barthes asks himself:

> How does a love end?—Then it does end? To tell the truth, no one—
> except for the others—ever knows anything about it; a kind of inno-
> cence conceals the end of this thing conceived, asserted, *lived* accord-
> ing to eternity.[4]

---

[4] *A Lover's Discourse—Fragments* (London: Jonathan Cape, 1979), p. 101.

We would never be able to love if we remained aware that love is transitory. There is no age when we outgrow this self-deceit, because it is in the very nature of love to inspire a sense of eternity.

The fact that happy moments can be recalled, that fulfillment can be relived—even if attenuated by time and space—proves that no love has ever been entirely futile. But most of all, however much rancor we may feel, we must acknowledge that the old relationship is still present within us, in what it made of us. True enough, its end made us aware of our incompleteness and nailed us to our inadequacy; it made us aware of the impossibility of being fulfilled. But it had all the healthy violence of a weaning, and thus was also a conquest. *That* must be set down to the credit of love.

At this point we must distinguish between one break-up and another. There can be an active ending—I am the one to leave the other —in which case the end of the affair has for me a dynamic function. I am projected outward, I see the world as a hunting ground in which I hope to recover as soon as possible the exaltation I once experienced in the relationship I am leaving. But what if the rupture is passive?

It is in the nature of life that we should be fated to experience alternately one and the other of these two possible endings. Only in being left do we have the sense of failure. When I am abandoned I imagine I have not given enough or been everything I should have been to the other. I ask myself: What did I do? What should I have done? Why was I unable to manage this situation? And here the specter of death is instantly raised.

This is the moment when one wants to die or hopes for some fatal disease or accident because the idea that one's own inadequacy caused the separation is unbearable. This is difficult to live with. The tragic acts, the suicides, are attributable to this. It is difficult to intervene in these situations with any kind of consolation because there are no arguments capable of acting on the deep core of the personality that has taken the blow. The meaning and value of being, resident in the ego, have been thwarted. No other loss—not that of job or property or a loved one who is not one's partner—can destroy a human being like the end of love can, precisely because it made us feel alive and authentic.

Rilke said that silence is the one true proof of love, but it can also indicate the absence of feeling. Observe a couple in whom a rupture has occurred: the lack of life is indicated by the absence of dialogue. It is the silence of a ghost town. Where there is no fracture, we feel, even in silence, the harmony that flows between two souls—a mute but eloquent counterpoint. But the silence that follows abandonment is opaque, empty, without resonance. And here, once again, we must have the courage to admit there is nothing we can do.

Abandonment, like death, cannot be evaded. We can invent our story, but only its beginning; we can never know how it will end. When we fall in love we start something that will soon get beyond our control and take its own course. Love contains the premises and the promises of eternity, but also the germ of annihilation.

The abandoned person is a real and true survivor, a witness to the ruin that has been worked within one's own soul. After the dramatic separation from a woman he had passionately loved, Cesare Pavese wrote in his diary: "One does not kill oneself for love of a woman. One kills oneself because a love, any love at all, reveals us in our nakedness, misery, helplessness, nothingness."[5] One might speak of cruelty but life, objectively, is not cruel; it is only our perception that dubs it so.

The happiness we enjoy by the side of the loved one is a gift, but one with a cost. The price we pay is the despair that afflicts us at the

---

[5] *Il mestiere di vivere* (The Art of Living) (Turin: Einaudi, 1952), p. 400.

end. This, in turn, does not merely settle the accounts and close the books on the affair; it also represents the premise, the basis, on which to build a new life that contains in itself all of our past. In our painful awareness of the need to love someone despite the risk of abandonment, we become adults, even while preserving our infantile capacity to always raise questions about ourselves.

We are what we are thanks to what we have been. And what we have been includes our old despairs and new joys. We experience each of our loves as if it and it alone could gratify us, and so our restless eyes incessantly seek confirmation in the eyes of the other. In every single union we find a grain of the eternal, just as there is also, ineluctably, the shadow and ultimately death. We know very well that things come to an end but we live them as if they endured forever. And we cannot do otherwise, because each of us bears within the desire for the infinite.

The only true gratification lies not in any particular experience but in the fact of having had it and been changed because of it. In this perennial confrontation between the absolute and the contingent, heaven and earth, the eternal and the transitory, lies the drama and the greatness of human destiny.

> My yoke, alas, is never lifted from
> My shoulders, and my hurts are ever burning,
> And in my eyes the tears are springing still.
> Alas, it was my will
> To carve the unearthly grace
> Of her most lovely face
> In the immutable matter of my heart.
>
> —Petrarch, Ode 5, from the *Canzoniere.*

In my craft or sullen art
Exercised in the still night
When only the moon rages
And the lovers lie abed
With all their griefs in their arms,
I labour by singing light
Not for ambition or bread
Or the strut and trade of charms
On the ivory stages
But for the common wages
Of their most secret heart,

Not for the proud man apart
From the raging moon I write
On these spindrift pages
Nor for the towering dead
With their nightingales and psalms
But for the lovers, their arms
Round the griefs of the ages,
Who pay no praise or wages
Nor heed my craft or art.

—Dylan Thomas, "In My Craft or Sullen Art."

10
Solitude and Creativity

One could say that we are congenitally predisposed to suffer, even though it is probably wrong to impute to nature this discouraging condition that contradicts the instinct for self-preservation. More likely it is millenia of culture that have contaminated the will to live. Whatever the reason, it is a fact that human suffering is pervasive, sometimes imperceptible but at other times so brutally in evidence as to override all else.

Let it be clear that I am no friend of pain, but wherever we look it is there. To echo Kierkegaard:

> I am not the man who thinks that we ought never to suffer; I despise this paltry wisdom, and if I have a choice I prefer to bear pain to the bitter end. Suffering is beautiful, and there is vigor in tears; but one should not suffer like a man without hope.[1]

Human suffering has not only its shocking aspects, but also those of a more discrete nature that nevertheless carry significant weight. Loneliness, for example. We know well enough what it is, but only when we experience it personally does it touch us deeply. Isolation, like other emotional experiences, reaches a threshold beyond which words lose their meaning. We cannot communicate our most intimate experiences to others. And this is not due to the physical absence of people around us, but rather, paradoxically, to their presence. It makes itself felt the moment we are in contact with others, when we believe we ought to feel their nearness and support, but don't.

Thus we conclude that our loneliness is not due to a difficulty in having relationships but is rather a question of inner suffering that

---

[1] *Aut-Aut* (Either/Or) (Milan: Mondadori, 1956), p. 117.

can be neither cured nor alleviated by external presences. We become tragically aware of solitude as a basic human condition.[2]

One reason for that sense of alienation goes back to our most formative moments when essential needs like mirroring and tenderness were not met. When such deep desires are not gratified, one is obliged to create within oneself the response that others were not able to give. It is this surrogate fulfillment in the world of the imagination that makes us aware for the first time of our innerness. In other words, on both the ontogenetic and philogenetic levels, frustration motivates creative fantasy and with it the awareness of one's inner dimension. To acquire this knowledge means in a certain sense to become capable of understanding one's personal truth. This is always mute. When it is expressed, it is communicated in silence. If one really has to speak, what results is a *translation of silence.*

The contact with solitude allows us to avoid indoctrination; in fact, to create a complete *Weltanschauung* in this situation would mean deriving one's knowledge of reality exclusively from within. That is why, for example, it is so difficult for some children to start school. That which is proffered now clashes with something more vital and individual.

But at this point we make another tragic discovery: we learn that the world outside does not belong to us. In life's difficult moments we are always alone, because the other has no power to help us, however much he or she may want to. In such a predicament not even an invitation to conquer the outside world proves of interest. Sometimes the commitment to acquiring material wealth can be a defense against the deep fear of remaining alone. When we give up such external defenses, we enter a realm where we can no longer participate on the collective level because of our irreprehensible indi-

---

[2] See F. Fromm-Reichmann, "Loneliness," in *Journal for the Study of Interpersonal Processes,* vol. 22, no. 1.

vidualism. A person who lives consciously and intensely is considered dangerous by the collective because this is the very level on which truths are gathered.

In solitude—understood not as detachment from others but as a feeling of being alone among our fellows—we represent a truth that can unmask and denounce the falsity that circulates in the external world. The great figures in history, those who changed our vision of the world, drew their truths from the wells of their solitude.

One must not, of course, fool oneself into thinking there is no price to be paid for this. On the contrary, the price is very high: the suffering one feels when one tries to communicate and becomes aware of the distance between oneself and others. This totally personal experience cannot be translated into words, but it is as binding on us as an intimate secret. Many existential tragedies are due to this kind of life, one that offers us the opportunity of making our own the most intimate and profound aspects of things, but deprives us of human warmth and relationships. Every time we mingle in the community, in social situations, the flimsiness of conventional relationships is brought home to us.

A conventional relationship is not a substitute for, but the exact opposite of, an authentic one. The words it uses are virtually empty and have no expressive power. Such relationships are common in everyone's life, and so we live an almost uninterrupted sequence of exchanges that could be called insignificant if it were not for our few desperate attempts to save at least the semblance of a real bond. Even when the chance for an authentic relationship presents itself, we are so out of the habit and unprepared for it that the fear of being inadequate pushes us into adopting false behavior.

Thus we find ourselves in a dead-end street: on the one hand our relationships are conventional, false and painful; on the other, we have authentic ties that also make us suffer because they demand attitudes difficult to sustain. In a true relationship, what we are afraid of expressing is not our thoughts, because these, like social chatter, don't touch us, don't involve us on an intimate level. Our fear is rather for our feelings, which experience has taught us are generally trampled on. Yet they represent the truest expression of our being. It is only in the motion of our souls that we are authentic, and this is always the fruit and the elaboration of an intimate experience.

When we find ourselves involved in an authentic relationship, where one is expected to give free reign to one's most secret emotions, we are conditioned by the past and by the fear that our sensibilities will be derided. We would like to share our deepest truths but we are afraid of exposing them to a world different from our own. It is common, then, to experience loneliness just because we anticipate that the most personal expressions of our being would be misunderstood or incomprehensible to the other.

True communication is impossible not because we lack words, but because we have constructed a psychic life with absolutely individual values that have no external points of reference. We ourselves constitute the only referent and therefore every message misses its mark. Sentiments can express truth, but we do not always succeed in saying what we really want to, and so, frequently, we choose a false expedient. It is very hard, for example, to reveal to a partner a change in our feelings. In fact, it is so painful that we generally prefer to remain alone and silent, and then our whole life contradicts that unexpressed inner truth.

To be involved with another person means to participate in his or her inner life. But just this kind of experience in our formative years, remote perhaps and even forgotten, has left its mark. A kind of imprinting has made us panic at subsequent emotional experiences and has taught us once and for all that the only salvation—exactly like that first time—lies in acquiring psychological autonomy.

That is why we value psychological independence so highly. One can describe it in many ways, but its effect is always the same—emotional detachment from the attitudes of others, coupled with extreme sensitivity to one's own inner events. Thus the need for approval and affection from the outside is done away with. One nourishes oneself.

I am not referring here to the arid condition that results when one loses empathy with others or with human existence in its wider sense. Rather it is a question of acquiring a type of freedom that allows us to draw on inner resources for the strength we need for our own psychic well-being, while still being available to our fellows. In an early phase of life, it is the smile of another which gratifies; in a more mature state, that smile can still make us happy but our frame of mind and our strength do not depend on it.

Schools of wisdom vary on the road to be taken, but they agree on the final goal: whether it is called serenity or indifference to human affairs, imperturbability or insensitivity to pain, Ataraxia or Nirvana, the climax of human growth is always seen as a state of emancipation from passions, desires and inauthentic needs. But this goal can only be reached by passing through the painful knowledge that our deepest and most individual essence, just because of its uniqueness, is incomprehensible to others.

In each of us there are needs that conflict with traditional or collective standards, so that what may be valid in general is not necessarily valid for any particular individual. How do we know this? We need only ask ourselves. Then we immediately see that what we want and what we are is often quite different from the models the worlds offers. In a relationship, for example, we may express a need that seems strange because it has no counterpart in the experience of the other. Since our subjectivity is the very source of the need, that should be enough to justify our request. Alas, it seldom is.

The most disturbing aspect of this condition is the feeling of not being present. If we are used to considering others as being witnesses to our existence, there is a risk that whenever we can no longer count on such testimony we feel lost, we fear we have been canceled out. We feel this whenever we experience the loss of a loved one: the eyes whose look kept me alive have been closed and now it is I who no longer exist.

Thus we can reach another conclusion: the feeling of loneliness is itself a message of a deep need, and to experience it intensely and dramatically inspires us to seek out what is missing. From this point of view, loneliness itself becomes an opportunity for the conquest of new horizons that might stimulate a capacity for communication that the previous situation did not. I believe this capacity is latent in everyone and can be realized in artistic expression. One cannot compose a poem when one is too involved in life, for outer existence affords too much gratification: there is no need to do or say anything original. I am not saying that the ideal situation for artistic creation is privation, frustration and despair. It is true that exceptional sensitivity can make an individual more vulnerable, and consequently unhappy, and can even make one an artist, but these are two separate effects and it is an error to consider the former the cause of the latter. Nevertheless, the experience of solitude is a vital factor—necessary if not sufficient—for artistic expression.

There are no words adequate to voice our sense of alienation, but there is another way in which we may be permitted to express it. If in our early life we know we are loved, there is a good chance that later on we can experience solitude as a creative opportunity. Creative here does not only mean artistic but also refers to the ability to give birth to something new in ourselves.

In almost everyone's life there is a moment when one discovers one's uniqueness. It is of great psychological importance, this moment of awakening. By deepening this experience we learn how precious the life of a single human being is. Because of a series of environmental and hereditary factors, every living creature has some absolutely inimitable characteristics. That is why the life of the individual must be defended at all costs: in that one person, and in no one else, there is a unique quality that can bear unsuspected and unimaginable fruits.

Sensitive parents are aware of this. Unfortunately the needs and strictures of the collective do real violence to personal uniqueness. We are thrown into a world of rules and superficial relationships where psychologically leveling reigns, hence we must be on the lookout for some way in which to reveal the deepest springs of our individuality.

The creative reaction itself legitimizes the sense of loneliness that is foretold in our earliest moments. In infancy such an experience is doubly painful, because the capacity to experience loneliness is not accompanied by the ability to reach out to another. In these moments we realize some important truths. For example, to be detached from others is to be deprived of their help in communicating. This is when, Jung suggests, we create a secret life. In *Memories, Dreams, Reflections*,[3] he speaks of the importance of having a secret, for it renders the individual richer and more attentive to the world of inner feeling. While verbal communication is associated with Logos, the world of the secret (and hence of silence) is tied up with Eros, the realm of emotions.

The feeling of loneliness is one of the essential characteristics of the human condition, one that propels us toward new conquests. The products that emerge from the experience of isolation become tools to demolish the constricting forms of our existence. Therefore creative

---

[3] New York: Pantheon Books, 1961, p. 342.

activity can be construed as a new paradigm, born of the very contradictions of life.

In the process of development the individual has need of unequivocal messages; before reaching maturity, in fact, we are not in possession of categories for understanding the ambivalence of life. Life presents itself in polar opposites, but as children we cannot tolerate ambiguity. According to the theories of Melanie Klein this becomes clear to us at the most tender age, during the period of nursing, when the infant experiences gratification and frustration alternately. So from the very first we are subject to painful contradictions.

Ambiguity has a destabilizing effect. It is like standing before a road sign that shows both right and left as the direction to the same place. Life too, when we really live it, presents us with similar situations, creating worry and conflict. Individuals can respond to conflict situations in various ways. The majority opt for one of the two available alternatives, negating the other and thus withdrawing from the conflict, but in this way damaging their own ideas and feelings. Very few have the courage or the strength to hold the tension between opposites until a completely new standpoint emerges. Indeed, most people are afraid of the resulting crisis if they acknowledge there may be an equally valid alternative solution to a particular problem.

Think of religious conflicts. In order to establish itself a religious idea must deny the validity of all others. The most dangerous are the monotheistic beliefs because these, by definition, allow for only one God. The more unequivocal the ideas embraced, the more intolerance grows. The solution would be to admit that the same objective can be reached from different directions. Only those who can tolerate the existence of several possibilities, without fanatically championing any one, will develop in a creative manner. This is because, in acknowledging contradictory truths, one has to create an inner equilibrium to keep from being torn in two.

A solitary person who has penetrated to the bottom of certain realities inspires fear. He or she becomes the interpreter of something very profound that opposes collective superficialities. Profound truth is always contradictory, just as a great love is always ambivalent. Passion makes us capable of giving our lives for the other, but also of taking the life of the beloved. There are no two ways about it: where there is no conflict, neither is there love.

It is precisely in the experience of loneliness, therefore, that the creative process takes root. Inner desperation becomes a stimulus to understanding the meaning of what one is going through. The creative person has learned there are no absolutes, no stable points of reference: everything can be right and wrong at the same time. This knowledge makes it impossible to communicate with those for whom there is still a clear difference between what is right and what is wrong, between truth and deception.

At this point, in fact, we are functioning on two completely different levels. That which others tell us does not correspond to our inner perceptions, and so, in order to go on living, we are obliged find nourishment and support within ourselves.

—Yet many a gem lies hidden still
Of whom no pick-axe, spade, or drill
The lonely secrecy invades;

And many a flower to heal regret,
Pours forth its fragrant secret yet
Amidst the solitary shades.

—Baudelaire, from "Ill Luck."

I wake and feel the fell of dark, not day.
What hours, O what black hoürs we have spent
This night! what sights you, heart, saw; ways you went!
And more must, in yet longer light's delay.
    With witness I speak this. But where I say
Hours I mean years, mean life. And my lament
Is cries countless, cries like dead letters sent
To dearest him that lives alas! away.

    I am gall, I am heartburn. God's most deep decree
Bitter would have me taste: my taste was me;
Bones built in me, flesh filled, blood brimmed the curse.
    Selfyeast of spirit a dull dough sours. I see
The lost are like this, and their scourge to be
As I am mine, their sweating selves; but worse.

                    —Gerard Manley Hopkins.

11
Suffering and Humiliation

Why do we so often cause each other to suffer? It is legitimate to ask if evil exists and we should not be afraid to admit that one often encounters wickedness. Artists have well understood that evil is not only present in the world, but that it often wins out. Thus Shakespeare writes: "All men are bad and in their badness reign."[1]

In general we are fairly ready to accept any act of nature, however terrible. What is really hard to bear is what is done to us by people. We suffer most of all when we are misunderstood, abused or belittled. Generally others perceive us in a way that overlooks the bulk of our inner world. Metaphorically we could say that a bad person is blinded by the light but, like a nocturnal animal, manages to see very well in the darkness, in that specific darkness that seems to comprehend all of our being. When we are seen in this partial way, we run the risk of no longer feeling ourselves to be whole because we become incomplete objects for ourselves.

In order to gain the upper hand, wickedness must first split us into fragments and weaken us; it never attacks our troops in full force but first seeks to disperse them by deliberately focusing on a single aspect. Our defense consists in paying continual attention to ourselves and not becoming accomplices in this fragmenting process.

We must admit that the external world, the collective, is very clever at recognizing one's weak spot, one's shadow side. That is the most questionable area of the personality, but also the most interesting and vital. In any human relationship that involves conflict, it is always the shadow that is attacked, our least defensible aspect.

---

[1] Sonnet 121.

When this happens, there are two ways to defend ourselves. In the first place, we must realize that what is being attacked really exists in us and is not an invention of the other. In the second place, we must recognize that a specific attitude is required on our part. In fact, it is essential not to accept the attacks of others passively but to defend oneself actively.

Slightly different, but psychologically no less important, is the question of the attitude one takes toward oneself. On an objective level, being attacked at our weak point may require an aggressive and defensive attitude, but with regard to our inner selves it requires a dialogue and reconciliation with that negative aspect that has been made the target, for it is precisely this hidden part that is the source of our vitality.

The taller a tree is, the deeper its roots. Similarly, the greatness of an individual is proportionate to the depths of his or her roots. The more a person is externally limpid, good, perfect, the more diabolical the root. This is a psychological law we must always keep in mind. A person is saintly inasmuch as he or she continually confronts the possibility of being a demon.

If we do not know our own inner depths, we risk identifying with the darkness attributed to us. The attacker is not lying, because from the outside it is easy to perceive the weakest and most defenseless aspect of another. But it is a mistake to think that one trait represents our whole way of being, giving us an exclusively negative image. Instead of feeling like a tree in its totality, with branches and foliage, we feel ourselves to be only a decaying root. The worst psychological error is precisely in taking the part for the whole—identifying with our shadow.

When a person has directed a spotlight onto a single facet of our personality and succeeded in making us look like a monster, we feel intensely misunderstood. This is not all bad, for it forces us into isolation and directs us toward our essential task: self-knowledge. This is a process lasting a lifetime; one's achievements are never definitive but must always be renewed.

In myths and fables with the theme of the hero's journey it is always the weakest child, the dummling, who leaves the parental home and experiences solitude. Only in the truth of our inner world can we learn that the trait others have identified as a defect is really indispensable to our individuality.

But just here we face great dangers. This is the time when one is either crucified or declared mad. The archetypical motif of the crucifixion shows that those who accept their evil as an integral part of themselves are inconvenient for the collective because the dark side always goes against the moral laws of the time. Whoever breaks them must be neutralized. The history of human thought is littered with lives that have ended at the stake, on the cross or in an insane asylum.

We also face this threat when our particular genius is obvious to others. To have genius generally means to have the capacity for seeing things in a completely new light and notably in advance of others. The great discoveries are the fruit of thought; the mind is always superior to concrete facts because it can intuit new possibilities and modes of existence. Think of the sun that appears to move before our eyes: it was genius that recognized this as an inaccurate collective perception.

Wickedness quite often has a collective character, hence we must never lose sight of our individual uniqueness. This is the most important truth to grasp: a person such as I has never before existed and can never exist again; why then suffocate this unique individuality with collective values?

To grasp the multiple realities of being one must have a special kind of courage. Whoever defies the rules by expressing his or her own ideas not only displays an inner light but also the shadow. One must be audacious enough to consciously live one's shadow side, otherwise one really and truly sins against oneself—a sin that can never be forgiven. The basic question we must ask ourselves in drawing up the balance sheet of our lives is this: "Did I live as I really was?" If I cannot answer yes, I have not truly lived.

Our greatest achievements are often those that start out by frightening us. Goethe tells us that Mephistopheles represents "a power that would/Alone work evil, but engenders good."[2] It is as if Mephistopheles crossed our path and we had to look him in the face. This is the kind of courage that generates a series of envious attacks by others.

Another danger in such situations is that we are gripped by guilt. It is as if we felt guilty for having succeeded where others failed; it is that vague sensation we get when faced with our capacity for self-realization compared to those who have come to a halt.

The guilt feelings that arise in us when we acquire independence derive from our experience as infants. We all try to emancipate ourselves from the absolute and undifferentiated bond with the parental figures. We try to break away from this original satellite status to become the center of attraction for a new constellation. This is no easy task because it is far from simple to renounce the protection of the parents. Hence even as adults most of us continue to need the approval of others.

The first steps toward independence are always regarded with justified apprehension. In the world of nature a too precocious autonomy can lead to death, and in the human realm it often leads us astray and creates confusion. This is why the self-sufficiency of children is always kept limited and why, on the interpersonal level, a network of

---

[2] *Faust* (London: Penguin, 1986), p. 75.

regulations is created that controls and also protects the life of the individual.

The sense of guilt is often activated by what Heidegger calls "idle talk,"[3] a common way of evaluating others without using one's head. Idle talk is not founded on personal experience but on ready-made judgments and collective opinion. It eliminates the need for personal evaluation. On the psychological level, idle talk cannot appreciate a person as one whose experience is unique. On the contrary, it prejudges according to what one ought to be, and finds the other wanting.

Psychological development requires the differentiation of oneself from collective stereotypes. One cannot recognize oneself in a generalization. In fact, any idea or rule that cannot be verified on the individual level must be thrown out. Here we can identify the real problem in our relations with others: they are always constrained by the needs of the collective. Of course, from time to time we all get caught up in external values, mindlessly parroting rules rather than thinking for ourselves. If we observe ourselves in the course of a day, we realize just how often, even involuntarily, we express judgments that are not really the fruit of personal reflection.

What is it that pushes us to judge others not according to their essence but by collective prejudices? It cannot be simple distraction. There is a deeper need, the need to project onto the other a judgment we cannot accept for ourselves. We can only face certain diabolical aspects of ourselves by seeing them at a distance. If we do not confront our shadow we will always tend to project its characteristics. It is easier to see the demon in others than in oneself.

Many of us belong to a religious tradition where life itself is the expiation of an atavistic guilt, and the roots of our personal suffering

---

3 *Being and Time* (London: Basil Blackwell, 1988), p. 211.

often grow from these beliefs. It seems that the destiny of each of us recreates the destiny of God's most beautiful angel. Lucifer, the "bearer of light," was condemned to darkness. His light is no longer visible. In daring to be authentic, we are cast by others in the same role—from being bearers of light, we become bearers of darkness. Thus the enemy renders us opaque.

Relating to the world actually does bring out our worst aspects. As soon as we are labeled in a negative way, we *become* negative. Our actions take on a dark character. Over the course of years, we construct a model whose truth rests on the imaginings of others and not on our actual experience. Though times have changed since Lucifer, it is not inappropriate even today to speak of persecution. A person who feels continually persecuted is said to be paranoid, but this feeling often has a basis in reality.

The opposition between discrimination and blind acceptance, between individual and collective, has always existed. History shows that what today appears to be blasphemy and sacrilege can become tomorrow's faith. But who is capable of committing a complete sacrilege? And who is capable of totally embracing a faith?

Here we come to the theme of humiliation. In the subtle and perfidious dynamics of human relationships, there is a perverse psychological law that has its origins in the sense of inferiority we each have. We fight against it and try to overcome it by being active. But, unfortunately, many think the only way to feel superior is to belittle others.

In Hawthorne's novel *The Scarlet Letter,* a young woman in seventeenth-century America commits adultery and bears a child as a result. Both are exposed to public view from a platform in front of the entire community while the pastor castigates the adulteress. She is separated from the community and obliged to live with her daughter in a house on the edge of society, making do with whatever people are disposed to pay her for embroidery. And she must wear on her breast a large scarlet letter A as a perennial reminder of her guilt. But the psychological force of the situation lies in the fact that the pastor who violently condemned and humiliated her was in fact the lover who fathered her child. Just so, in humiliating another we are actually pinpointing something we share with our victim.

To humiliate involves pointing out something of which one is ashamed. This may be done for plausible reasons, but the true objective is the moral destruction of the individual. Those who make a habit of humiliating others see only their petty and mediocre aspects. But they themselves are the truly mediocre ones because they cannot perceive what greater values might be there.

If it is really necessary for a negative judgment to be made, it should be made on what we really are and not on what we ought to be. But mediocre people are always waiting to catch us just at this point, on a level where we have no desire or ability to express ourselves. Rilke describes a more noble endeavor:

> Ever since I was a child I believe I have prayed for *my* problem alone, that I might be granted mine and not by mistake that of the carpenter, or the coachman, or the soldier, because I want to be able to recognize myself in my problem.[4]

Those who humiliate us strike at our self-respect. However well we may know our defects, we tend to present others with an ideal image, a persona. But when we are humiliated we are deprived of the mask that covers our shameful sides. Thus humiliation brings up the problem of the shadow. All that we reject or repress in ourselves is brought to light and judged.

To be stripped naked, literally or metaphorically, is always humiliating. There are parts of our bodies we don't expose to others for

---

[4] *Letters to a Young Poet* (New York: Vintage Books, 1986), p. 77.

fear of being judged. Similarly, when someone uncovers our inner-most secrets, we feel powerless. We are at the mercy of anyone who can penetrate with cruel and indiscreet gaze the most hidden and painful corners of our souls.

Edith Jacobson has described the effect of humiliating treatment on political prisoners in Nazi Germany:

> The prisoners woke up at night, feeling that their limbs or their faces did not belong to them. They would anxiously touch the es-tranged body parts, trying to recover the feeling of intactness of their body self. During the day they were suddenly overcome by frighten-ing experiences of psychic self-estrangement; with feelings of being outside their self and of watching themselves think, talk or act, as though they were another person, and the like.[5]

This is the evil consequence of humiliation: alienation from oneself, with the victim being aware of it, made to feel diminished.

Humiliations are frequent in childhood and often defended as a le-gitimate form of upbringing. Whole generations have been raised in the shadow of the prejudice that humiliation is necessary to make a mature adult. Ingmar Bergman has spoken at length of the degrading treatment he suffered in childhood. His home life came to a dramatic end when he punched his father and slapped his mother. The theme of humiliation pervades his work. In the film *Passion* the main char-acter speaks of past humiliations as of still-open wounds; in *Fanny and Alexander* there is the scene in which the pastor beats the child in front of the whole family.

A friend of mine tells about his home town (a small place in Sicily) where a certain child, whenever he did something bad, was undressed by his mother and tied to a chair set out in the street. Passing adults made jokes about his small penis. Today this boy is a criminal who has been in jail several times. In Werner Herzog's *The*

---

[5] *Depression* (New York: International Universities Press, 1971), p. 143.

Ballad of Stroszek, the hero tells of his childhood in an orphanage during the Nazi period. When he wet his bed he was forced to stand holding the sheet stretched out until it dried. Bergman says that for the same offense he was obliged to wear a red skirt.

For a long time humiliation was considered a valuable teaching method. Well-known university professors discouraged and insulted their students in front of the whole class. A famous journalist tells how during his apprenticeship at an important newspaper, the managing editor called him in to say he had written a very bad piece. He did not explain what was wrong with it but simply tore it up in his face in front of other editors and threw the pieces into the air.

Authoritarian regimes use an official form of humiliation that is vicious and crude. The Italian Fascists gave large doses of castor oil to their adversaries and then drove them around on trucks, slipping and sliding in their own excrement.

In insane asylums, prisons and the military, humiliation is an important component of the repressive structure. Think of the degrading searches a person is put through on entering prison. In Italy even court trials have a humiliating aspect, with the defendant on view in a glass box like an animal in a cage. In the past, corporal punishment was inflicted on soldiers before all the troops, especially assembled for the occasion. Newspapers have recently reported cases of suicide among young draftees who were forced by the regulars to lick the bathroom floor or the shoes of their comrades.

Humiliation is frequently depicted in films. In Stanley Kubrick's *A Clockwork Orange,* the hero, a violent young criminal, is in the end deconditioned. The psychiatrists proudly demonstrate the results by having the youth lick their boots. In *An Officer and a Gentleman,* a group of trainees are continually taunted by their sergeant. One finally hangs himself. In *Full-Metal Jacket,* the humiliated draftee turns on his sergeant and kills him, then shoots himself.

Under Christianity humiliation becomes a kind of victory of the weak. "He who humbles himself shall be exalted," "Blessed are the meek and the poor in spirit because they shall see the kingdom of Heaven." The humiliation of the flesh is a Catholic practice, apparent in the various hair shirts worn by saints and monks.

At bottom, humiliation is an instrument of power. If someone represents a danger, there are two ways of neutralizing the threat: physical elimination or humiliation. If you destroy a person through humiliation, you have him or her under your thumb. Having lost human dignity, the victim can no longer harm you.

But we must also consider a more subtle effect: the more a person is humiliated, the more do feelings of guilt in the humiliators gradually disappear. Thus Franz Stangl, head of the Treblinka extermination camp, when asked the reason for all the humiliations and tortures inflicted on those destined to be killed, replied: "To condition those who were directly employed in carrying out our operation. . . . To make it possible for them to do what they were doing."

Thou who abruptly as a knife
Didst come into my heart; thou who,
A demon horde into my life,
Didst enter, wildly dancing, through

The doorways of my sense unlatched
To make my spirit thy domain—
Harlot to whom I am attached
As convicts to the ball and chain,

As gamblers to the wheel's bright spell,
As drunkards to their raging thirst,
As corpses to their worms—accurst
Be thou! Oh, be thou damned to hell!

I have entreated the swift sword
To strike, that I at once be freed;
The poisoned phial I have implored
To plot with me a ruthless deed.

Alas! the phial and the blade
Do cry aloud and laugh at me:
"Thou art not worthy of our aid;
Thou art not worthy to be free.

Though one of us should be the tool
To save thee from thy wretched fate,
Thy kisses would resuscitate
The body of thy vampire, fool."

  —Baudelaire, "The Vampire."

They that have the power to hurt and will do none,
That do not do the thing they most do show,
Who, moving others, are themselves as stone,
Unmoved, cold, and to temptation slow;
They rightly do inherit heaven's graces,
And husband nature's riches from expense;
They are the lords and owners of their faces,
Others but stewards of their excellence.
The summer's flower is to the summer sweet,
Though to itself it only live and die,
But if that flower with base infection meet,
The basest weed outbraves his dignity:
For sweetest things turn sourest by their deeds;
Lilies that fester smell far worse than weeds.

—Shakespeare, Sonnet 94.

12

The Desire for Power

The search for success is generally motivated by the specter of failure. I don't think people exist who are not possessed by this phantom, especially in adolescence when insecurity is particularly intense. If an individual cannot tolerate the idea of defeat, life takes on the form of an unceasing battle to negate and exorcise it. This creates a strong, implicit enmity between people. It is the root of much human suffering and we encounter it everywhere.

We must distinguish between the need to dominate and the use of power for a common goal. It is possible to assume power temporarily, as the Roman Cincinnatus did, for the public good, when he was called into battle. He wielded limited power for a particular purpose and then returned to his normal life. In domination, we have instead power for power's sake, the desire for supremacy over others.

When one speaks of dominating others, one must think not only of the large-scale examples such as dictatorships, but of something we all experience. The most common and insidious exercise of power in fact takes place between individuals. In love relationships it expresses itself in the attempt to block the other's development.

One of the tap-roots of the need to exercise power is the unconscious sense of one's own inability to reach self-fulfillment. It springs from a feeling of impotence in the face of life. Clearly, this is not a characteristic of a creative individual, who feels swept along by a stream of life that has the vital dimensions of eternity. Such a person does not feel limited; what he or she does and thinks goes beyond the confines within which simple survivors are compelled to exist. In contrast, the person who seeks to dominate is bound to the question of personal survival.

The urge for domination not only tends toward absolute control, but also cannot tolerate the creativity of others. We see this operating on a larger scale in dictatorships, where it is always the arts that are attacked and those individuals with the most originality who are obliged to emigrate. Thus the creative person is the natural enemy of power.

Conversely, we must realize that when we express an original point of view we are bound to attract enemies. For those whose need is to dominate, the creative act is a serious threat for it represents the possibility of living rather than simply surviving. Those in command, those who hold the destinies of others in their hands, are continually faced with gestures that denounce their incapacity and sterility. And so any and every attitude that is a reminder of more ample possibilities is felt to be an injury.

The act of domination, both because it is spawned by a creative incapacity and because it leads to a drive to repress others' originality, is closely related to the fear of death. Human beings can have many passions—adventure, research, love—but only the lust for power requires the subjugation of others. As Canetti says of one who has the power of life or death over others:

> Each execution that he is responsible for lends him a certain strength: the strength of the survivor. His victims do not necessarily have to have formed ranks against him—they might have done so. His anxiety transforms them—perhaps only at a later date —into enemies who have fought against him. He has condemned them. They have been executed. He has survived them.[1]

The actions of such a person are in fact aimed at anulling the kind of life that would testify to his own dead condition. Solzhenitsyn speaks of Stalin in exactly these terms. Stalin believed a person could

---

[1] E. Canetti, *Crowds and Power* (London: Penguin, 1987), pp. 272-273.

only remain faithful for a limited length of time, after which he or she had to be eliminated:

> In cases of this kind his first thought was: for how long will it be possible to put faith in this man? And the second thought: Hasn't the moment already come to sacrifice him? . . . Lack of faith in people was his conception of the world.[2]

Creativity, on the other hand, fights against death, does not need to put others in chains, does not desire corpses or slaves. The difference between those driven by power and those who live creatively is that the former require the death of others as proof of their strength, while the latter can relate to others because they live autonomously.

When we meet an artistic personality we immediately notice the positive charge, just as we feel a negative atmosphere around those who exert power. Creativity means vitality not only for those who are themselves productive, but also for those who benefit indirectly. In a very significant statement, Jung says:

> If there were really nothing behind [one's actions] but collective standards of value on the one hand and natural instincts on the other, every breach of morality would be simply a rebellion of instinct. In that case valuable and meaningful innovations would be impossible, for the instincts are the oldest and most conservative element in man and beast alike. Such a view forgets the creative instinct which, although it can behave like an instinct, is seldom found in nature and is confined almost exclusively to *Homo sapiens*.[3]

Jean-Jacques Rousseau observed that man is born free but everywhere he is in chains. He was referring to social chains but the same is true when it comes to ties of a psychological kind. One psychological chain that binds us is the belief, albeit usually unconscious, that

---

2 A. Solzhenitsyn, *Il primo cerchio* (The First Circle) (Milan: Mondadori, 1974), pp. 146-147.

3 "Transformation Symbolism in the Mass," *Psychology and Religion,* CW 11, par. 390n.

we can only exist by manipulating others. There is no possibility of dialogue in such a situation; and it is only through dialogue that truth can emerge. Without dialogue, one identifies with an ideal; one feels one has the right and the duty to shape the other.

Lovers sometimes say, "You need me; you're nothing without me." This attitude cannot lead to an I-Thou dialogue. It underlies especially those relationships in which the partner is experienced exclusively as our own creation. One might call it the Pygmalion complex; it is more common than one would imagine. Remarks such as, "You are just what I always wanted," may seem to be expressions of love, but in reality they are dictated by a deep desire to mold the other, to hold his or her fate in one's hands.

The idea of power is closely connected to the idea of God. One's own image becomes divine; one loses a critical perspective on oneself and feels omnipotent. This is a highly destructive form of inflation. It is not in itself a pathological condition, because at times, especially in moments of danger, a sense of one's grandeur can be useful. But once an identification with omnipotence takes place, it is but a short step to the cruel domination of others.

At bottom, the desire for power springs from the need to overcome deep uncertainty about oneself and reveals a fear of life. This fear is often due to deprivations experienced in early childhood. Self-confidence is the product of a series of introjections that guide and support us in difficult situations and give us the feeling that someone is watching out for us. What really counts here is the interiorization of the image. There is no need for external reassurance, because one has created a powerful interior world from which one draws the strength to go on living.

It is the same psychological mechanism that sustains an athlete during a competition or an actor on the stage. One feels protected, as if by a guardian angel.

This feeling of not being alone is fundamental for human beings. Anyone in the happy condition of being able to say, "God is with me," never feels impotent or inferior, never feels unequal to life's situations, never has the need to exert power. Of course the really dangerous ones are those who mouth the words but do not believe them. Those who do exert power are those who seek externally something they do not find within: reassurance, self-confirmation and fulfillment. Similarly, those who embark on an endless series of love affairs are seeking external confirmation of their capacities.

The power drive can be truly diabolical. Whoever wields power offers security to a great many people who truly feel helpless and insecure. This is what nourishes demagogues. Both those who take control of their fellows and those who submit are moved by the same requirement: to liberate themselves from a condition of inner need.

This is the common matrix of institutional religions and authoritarian states. Europe went through the most terrible moment of its history by virtue of a precise mandate entrusted to two men who seemed to incarnate the function of leadership—Hitler and Mussolini. These men did not take over by force but came to power legally, inasmuch as they appeared at the time to correspond to deep needs.[4] Rather than finding a rational, critical and dialectical solution to their problems, appeal was made to the two dictators and to their sense of omnipotence to remove repressive conditions.

One should understand that not only is it impossible to free oneself from a condition of need, but it is not even desirable. Our needs, however urgent and sometimes painful, are the stimuli to understanding ourselves and the world around us. Any fulfillment we are lucky enough to attain spurs us on to further levels of gratification. The

---

[4] See Hans Kohut, *Self-Psychology and the Humanities* (New York: W.W. Norton & Co., 1978), p. 71.

need to eat, drink and make love, for example, is never exhausted, because after satisfying these needs biologically we search for other levels of satisfaction. The demagogue who promises liberation from need and conflict—an implicit but unfulfilled promise in one's relationship with the mother—is only offering an illusion to those hungry for security.

It is just through this illusion that power is able to enthrall. Hitler told the Germans they were a master race and promised he would create a long-lasting empire for them. The nation that gave birth to such giants as Goethe and Schiller believed words like these for ten years—words that could only satisfy extremely primitive needs. In Leni Riefenstahl's film *The Triumph of the Will*, Hitler tells German youth: "I will make of you men who have no fear of death."

Demagogues deceive us. In the face of existential problems only one attitude is possible, that which allows us to continually create our own lives. To liberate oneself, even illusorily, from necessity would mean to remove oneself from history and return to an earthly paradise where everything is made perfect without our intervention. This search for Eden is so intense that throughout the nineteenth century, when the great geographic explorations took place, tropical countries were truly considered the last paradises, where nature gave everything spontaneously.

In reality we are only free when we accept the possibility of remaining forever unsatisfied. In order to feel alive, to escape from futility and death, man must create with works and with ideas. Power frees one from need, but in this way it leads to death, because the lack of desire is death. The truly alive individual is one who creates and fights against the lure of nothingness. Those who have confronted and overcome despair can try to give others the benefit of their experience. But it is no use fooling ourselves; everyone must travel this road.

In our culture every effort is made to avoid conflict and eliminate pain. Social structures are oriented to the avoidance of suffering, anxiety and emptiness. And yet loss and failure are integral parts of life. Young people tend to imagine life as a series of victories: each conquest guarantees the next and the future is promising. As adults, however, we learn that any achievement is ephemeral. Its validity does not endure in time. Success is not an inheritance that pays interest you can live on. In the next moment we may have to risk our entire capital and possibly lose it. Our mental health is evidenced in part by how we relate to this reality.

The fear of not reaching the goals we set ourselves is thus tied to an idea of death conceived in terms of defeat. In fact, it is simply the end of a chapter; others follow. Failure and success can never be fully explained by specific factors because the two terms have no objective criteria on which to base exact evaluations of life's events. The great questions and the significant stages of life have different implications for each individual. All of us walk our existential paths with unique motives.

There are two possible responses to the feeling of failure: destructiveness or the will to persevere. Some are totally destroyed, while others find new energy and go on. When we feel broken by a defeat, it means we have identified ourselves completely with a particular goal. This is the condition that leads to thoughts of suicide. But our lives have more value than is reflected by any one achievement. Behind the limited appearances of concrete reality there is always a more ample richness. Indeed, the person who manages to maintain a certain detachment from external circumstances can actually be stimulated by defeat.

Only strong people know how to face defeat, but the word strong here should not be understood in its everyday meaning. What it refers to is the courage to experiment. Individuals who continually

seek and test unknown waters risk shipwreck, unlike those who
choose to remain on solid ground. Whether they are astronauts going
to the moon or young people leaving home for the first time, those
who dare must accept the possibility of failure. But they are also
stronger for having made the effort and survived. To have failed
means at least to have had the courage to try. Those who claim to
have never suffered defeat have never really lived.

Each of us has our unique dream compared with which collective
values are abstract and worthless. Lack of success has meaning only
on the subjective level. One knows when one has failed, even if
others see what appears to be a victory according to collective criteria. The individual is the only true arbiter, the only one who can give
meaning to what has occurred. Personal defeat can in fact become
fertile ground for future success if one gives it the propulsive meaning that can be derived from an intense investment of psychic energy.
Thus Rilke writes as follows:

> You have had many sadnesses, large ones, which passed. And you
> say that even this passing was difficult and upsetting for you. But
> please, ask yourself whether these large sadnesses haven't rather gone
> right *through* you. Perhaps many things inside you have been trans-
> formed; perhaps somewhere, someplace deep inside your being, you
> have undergone important changes while you were sad. The only
> sadnesses that are dangerous and unhealthy are the ones that we carry
> around in public in order to drown them out with the noise; like dis-
> eases that are treated superficially and foolishly, they just withdraw
> and after a short interval break out again all the more terribly; and
> gather inside us and are life, are life that is unlived, rejected, lost, life
> that we can die of.[5]

Poets have no need to study psychology or psychoanalysis in
order to express the profound truths of existence. Psychologists approach the soul from without; the poet from within. Rilke here em-

---

[5] *Letters to a Young Poet* (New York: Random House, 1984), pp. 81-82.

phasizes the futility of broadcasting one's anguish. Instead we should contain our suffering and remind ourselves that only those who have never lived are safe from failure. This is why one should evaluate apparent success as carefully as we eye defeat: neither may have anything to do with our authentic human qualities.

On our way toward psychological maturity there is a crucial moment, a fork in the road where we must not leave our choice to chance. One can choose the route that looks more comfortable, represented by compromise and the avoidance of unease. Or one can take the rockier and more difficult road of self-authenticity. The first road promises a pleasant walk; the second, high adventure. Those who choose compromise will follow a guided tour along well-beaten paths in a domesticated landscape. Whoever chooses the second way sets out on a solitary expedition into unexplored country, commonly indicated on ancient maps with the warning, *"Hic sunt leones"* (Here be lions). The beast the intrepid voyager could run into is none other than the devil or, in other terms, his own shadow.

For those who choose the path of personal truth, violent encounters with the shadow are not only inevitable but also precious. In those moments, reason, which seemed to be our greatest defense, is weakened and the irrational steps in. When the intellect goes soft and fails us, we must force ourselves to witness our weakness, to become more alert and alive than ever. We must enter into dialogue with the irrational. In the awareness that logic alone does not lead to understanding, we become more human .

I have said that the soul is not more than the body,
And I have said that the body is not more than the soul,
And nothing, not God, is greater to one than one's self is,
And whoever walks a furlong without sympathy walks to his
    own funeral drest in his shroud,
And I or you pocketless of a dime may purchase the pick
    of the earth,
And to glance with an eye or show a bean in its pod confounds
    the learning of all times,
And there is no trade or employment but the young man
    following it may become a hero,
And there is no object so soft but it makes a hub for the
    wheel'd universe,
And I say to any man or woman, Let your soul stand cool and
    composed before a million universes.

—Walt Whitman, *Leaves of Grass.*

13

Staying Aware

We each have our own story, unique and unrepeatable, like the individual patterns in a kaleidoscope. We must develop and cherish our sense of individuality or else we risk becoming animate beings without consciousness of self, merely bad copies of the world around us. This may seem obvious, and yet we know the effort required to resist the temptation to identify with external models. We must be constantly vigilant. We need only let down our guard for a moment and immediately we find ourselves mouthing collective judgments and prejudices. Only with constant attention to our own personal truth can we remain grounded and authentic.

In the realm of psychology there is a school of thought which says people can be programmed like computers. But we know there are limits to the power of conditioning. At bottom we have a hard core that others cannot dent, a residue of originality that, if only we seek it out, will be our salvation. This core is what one counts on during the process of analysis.

The recovery of our original individuality is a task we undertake regardless of all else and against the laws of nature. In our capacity as human beings we have often pursued goals contrary to those of nature, as evidenced by our acquired ability to defeat certain diseases. One might say we are born unconscious but with a unique potential. Whenever our attention lapses, the psychological level of civilization drops and impulses emerge which are properly called primitive. And we would still be living on that level if mankind had not invented culture. On the psychological level we have to use violence against our genetic inheritance. But, what is it that drives us to go against nature?

The fact that we concern ourselves with such issues is an indication of a general malaise. Those who don't feel dissatisfied do not ask these questions. The rest of us can only grope for the right words to describe the sickness of our time. I use the word sickness here not in its everyday sense; rather, it is a feeling of unfulfillment that assails us even when things are going well. To feel fully human, mere survival is not enough. The majority of modern psychological disturbances are in fact concerned with inner problems that plague us without keeping us from pursuing our usual activities.

Mental suffering is a cry of the soul, just as physical pain is a call for attention to the body. If we love without being loved in return, we suffer; but this suffering makes us aware that we have an inner life. In order to bear the pain we listen to music, read a book or take drugs; but it is all in vain because at that moment our soul is crying out and what it needs is for us to listen. Thus we must learn to communicate with ourselves in an individual manner, using a personal language.

The fundamental first step in living the existential moment authentically consists in affirming one's individual experience in its totality. Accepting one's own pain means to have understood that the path of one's existence cannot be made absolutely smooth: no one can avoid danger and injury. Only we ourselves can fight for our own lives, taking full responsibility for what we encounter along the way. The obstacles may take the form of illness, economic problems, attack, rejection, vexations of every kind. It is not by their quality or even their quantity that we can evaluate them, but by the psychic situation. There are those who flee from a danger and those who face it, and the courage to test ourselves against it is born in that very moment, thanks to the danger itself.

It may seem rhetorical to say that the obstacles themselves help us to grow, but on the psychological plane we can affirm that they stimulate expression of the inner dimension. Difficulties are structural elements of life. Just as the resistance of a piece of marble opposes the sculptor, we become stronger according to the degree we are tested. And it is here that we can forge our destinies; in these crucial situations we must ask ourselves what we have made and what we are making of our uniqueness.

These are hard questions to face, and even harder when we have already lived a great part of our lives. Have we been afraid that others will attack and humiliate us, defame and mistrust? Though these fears block expressions of individuality, we must see them as stumbling blocks put in our way to force us to preserve our individuality. Of course we run the risk of making mistakes, because the rules of the game are only learned in the very act of hacking out the path. The great scientific and humanistic works—those that completely change our conception of the world—are only possible because a single person stops looking in the same direction as everyone else. Obviously such innovators encounter obstacles, difficulties and unpredictable situations. But they go on.

Near the end of his life, Jung declared that when we follow the path of individuation we must take full account of our errors, because without them life would not be complete.[1]

The one true danger we all face, the one that synthesizes them all, comes from continuously adhering to our individual choice, because it has no external points of reference. The collective path has already been leveled by others, and thus you always know where you are going. The individual path, on the other hand, has numerous signposts but no indication of the "right" direction. When we accept the risk of choosing between contradictory solutions, we feel the life of

---

[1] *Memories, Dreams, Reflections* (New York: Pantheon Books, 1963), p. 358.

the soul. To be psychologically vital we must always fluctuate between poles. Every choice we make implies the sacrifice of other possibilities, and there is no one who can tell us if the choice is right or wrong.

To live in this way means to renounce those tablets of the law that govern collective existence and to interiorize all polarities and contradictions. It means to set in motion within oneself a process of judgment, evaluation, where accused and accuser are one. We struggle within ourselves, with no external guidelines, for the resolution of the dichotomy that tears us apart but at the same time makes us feel alive. In this condition there are no objective factors that can help. We live our inner drama in solitude.

To live in the world without acknowledgment from it requires a level of psychological development that is difficult to reach, especially at an early age. This explains why, even when we put our trust in an inner truth, we still live in a state of desire for some external reference point. We experience anxiety, or perhaps just a general fear of living.

In every other species there is a precise moment in which the cub ceases to be a cub and confronts the environment alone. This occurs when the animal's biological development allows it to survive independently. The period of dependence is fixed and lapses at a regular time because it is connected to the environment. This has remained more or less the same for millenia, with the exception of recent times when *homo sapiens* has taken on the job of remodeling the world. But apart from man's misdeeds, nature also introduces environmental variations: climatic changes, for instance, can render the cub's period of dependence absolutely insufficient and its weaning entirely premature. In these cases the species may become extinct or it may survive, saved by those individuals whose accidental characteristics make them more adaptable.

For humans the situation is not so simple. The moment we must face life by ourselves, we leave behind all those familiar references. We lose those who have done the thinking for us, thus relieving us of fear. In the course of our development we must abandon this protected environment, but the milieu we then find ourselves in is not a natural one; rather it is cultural.

Development thus requires the passage from a biological system to a cultural one. In the latter, innate abilities are no longer useful because the world is so changed that natural equipment no longer guarantees survival. The idea that difficulties diminish as we grow is based on the erroneous assumption that development is rooted in our genetic traits. But when speaking of the individual it is a question of both cultural and psychological development.

In the fear of living we find a generalized incapacity to receive what life, in an entirely indifferent manner, offers us. It almost seems that one hasn't the strength to bear the weight of existence. This experience is based on the assumption, often unconscious, that we should, like the animal cub, feel naturally part of life. But this premise is unfounded because by now there is nothing at all natural in a world that has become so essentially cultural as ours. In the larger animal kingdom, life unfolds in an almost automatic way; but this is not so in the human world.

It is not up to us to make value judgments; our duty is rather to be aware of the dichotomy. As Freud said, when we come face to face with reality we must struggle to change whatever can be changed and to accept with patience what cannot be modified. To which I would add that we must also think carefully. To wish that things should go a certain way is legitimate, but the reality of the world is quite another matter. Thus it is not nature we must fight against but the world of culture and its rules, which are not biologically given but must be learned step-by-step as we move through life.

It is not so much the laws of nature that are decisive but the norms and conventions of people, the superstructure we have erected on the fundamental biological base. The fear of life is the fear of confronting the world and testing oneself against its norms. A person who is courageous in the face of a natural danger may still be incapable of speaking in public. We are afraid of exposure on a social level; human rules shame us because we feel more acutely the fear of being judged. We are all afraid of this, but what differentiates us is the way we react.

We have to come to terms with reality and find a positive relationship to our fear. There is no other possibility, because however well equipped we may be, nature and culture are always stronger. The feeling of panic is always at hand, but our first job is to make contact with it, not to pretend it isn't there. Children can fool themselves, but as mature adults we cannot. In order not to succumb and remain paralyzed, we must enter into the very language of fear.

> Batter my heart, three-personed God, for you
> As yet but knock, breathe, shine, and seek to mend.
> That I may rise and stand, o'erthrow me and bend
> Your force to break, blow, burn, and make me new.
> I, like an usurped town to another due,
> Labor to admit you, but oh, to no end!
> Reason, your viceroy in me, me should defend,
> But is captivated, and proves weak or untrue.
> Yet dearly I love you and would be lovèd fain,
> But am betrothed unto your enemy.
> Divorce me, untie, or break that knot again,
> Take me to you, imprison me, for I,
> Except you enthrall me, never shall be free,
> Nor ever chaste except you ravish me.

> —John Donne, Sonnet 14.

14
The Hidden Truth

The facts of life almost always instill fear in us. In learning to relate to our fear we understand its language, albeit with difficulty because it is an imperfect and approximate code. When a creative person tries to delineate an inner image, for instance, the product is invariably far from the original intuition. This is why Plato said that in the last analysis the truth is inexpressible.[1]

True teaching takes place not only through particular creative forms, but also on some special wavelength. It does not bring glory or honors. The moment of knowledge is sufficient unto itself. Such moments happen in analysis when one comes to understand that the world of emotions has been much more meaningful in one's life than any other, and also that this knowledge must remain secret, hidden from profane eyes.

The meaning of fear cannot be grasped by our usual way of thinking. We must approach it with a psychological perspective. The therapy for a phobic person, for example, is gradually to accustom the individual to the phobic object, because it contains something that could reveal the meaning of the panic. The true object of terror is never clearly expressed. We must learn to translate it. And just as in the pathological situation the attempt to evade the fearful object ends as a flight from a whole series of experiences, so in normal circumstances the desire to avoid making contact with fear means to flee from life itself.

The reality of any personal relationship is like a poem, which can be rendered into another language in various ways, depending on the

---

1 *The Seventh Letter* (London: Penguin, 1988), 341 c/d, p. 136.

sensibilities of the translator. Based on our experience of life, we can either be translators or traducers of what we are trying to understand. Much harm is caused by an inadequate translation, for it keeps us from really understanding the text. Sometimes, if we are lucky, we are spurred to examine the original. Thus our view of the external world is a fluctuation between two poles—fidelity to the original text and a translation that may betray its meaning.

The origin of the possibility for error goes back to infancy. As one begins to learn a language, one misunderstands certain words. These subsequently become associated with ideas different from their intended meanings and determine the possibilities for our psychological development all the more for our not being conscious of them. If such precocious experiences have been badly translated, we will always face the world with an attitude of fear and will continue to misinterpret situations analogous to those that in infancy we could not translate accurately.

Infantile trauma stems from situations too complex for the child to understand. For instance, if an adult's caress, which a child is disposed to interpret as a sign of tenderness, should instead take on an aggressive or erotic character, the child goes through a traumatic experience. That is why a large part of psychological work involves returning to the past for another look at the original text, critically examining and retranslating early experiences. Childhood traumas can lead us to feel that life itself is against us, we will always be too feeble to defend ourselves. But the true difficulty springs from the lack of appropriate means for understanding a particular problem.

Just as science requires suitable equipment, so too does psychic life. The problems we encounter are primarily internal, related more to our instruments of observation than to the objects we observe. Thus we should try to reelaborate our experience in the only appropriate language, the one which offers us the means to move in the direction of life. In order to do this, we must understand that life is not a given fact, and that as a consequence we are obliged to reflect on its essence. Without such consideration we remain as unaware of our condition as does any dumb animal. As humans we have the obligation to overcome our ignorance and realize our individual potential. This is not given to us as a gift but must be independently and autonomously won.

A sculptor may know that a statue lies hidden in a piece of stone, but in order to reveal it he must have some idea of its form. Similarly, we require a basic intuition to guide our actions, to cut the shape of our individual lives from the impersonal cloth of existence. Once we have a clear perception of our inner life, it is our duty to salvage and express the things that fear has kept locked away. This is only possible if we know what to do with them. In a pathological condition we have no image of the statue, no life plan, and so we are cut off from the fundamental project hidden within us.

Jungian concepts offer an existential model that is synthesized in the process of individuation, by means of which an inwardly divided person without hope reacquires a unity in which conscious and unconscious converge.[2] It is through this process that one's unique inner design is discovered. Then one knows what to do.

The connection with one's inner life is essential for psychological growth. On the ontogenetic level it can coincide with the moment in which the child recognizes his or her own image in the mirror and becomes conscious of self. Only with the development of self-awareness can we understand what is truly important—the fact that nothing is *caused* by others. To see others as a cause is really and truly pathological because it displaces the internal conflict .

---

[2] See Aldo Carotenuto, *The Vertical Labyrinth: Individuation in Jungian Psychology* (Toronto: Inner City Books, 1985) and *The Spiral Way: A Woman's Healing Journey* (Toronto: Inner City Books, 1986).

Considerations of this kind do not, of course, exempt us from keeping an attentive eye on reality. The Nazi persecutions really did come from the outside. Such situations give us the chance to choose between intervention and nonintervention. I remember my teacher Bernhard, two days before his death, telling me he felt himself to be in a state of grace because he was doing all he could to save his life, but that he understood only God could help him. This is one way of accepting death as a part of life; but to do so one must fight until the very end. An aphorism of Marcello Marchesi comes to mind: "The important thing is that when death comes it finds us alive."

The way in which we interpret reality always has its basis in our inner world. This means that however hard we try to be objective, our image of the world is necessarily subjective. We are the ones who read it in that particular way, invest it with those special meanings, translate it in one way rather than another. Since we are psychological creatures, our relationship with the world and our knowledge of it always have a mental character and thus are thick with subjectivity. The beauty of a day, for instance, is not only a question of climate or landscape, it is also determined by our inner disposition.

Every attitude to the world depends upon an interior mediation; reality neither has it in for us nor takes our side. In a given situation help or hindrance may come to us from others, but it is foolish to suppose the world spends its time worrying about us. Therefore, in general, our adversaries are not the objective facts, the obstacles, everything that appears negative to us. Our true enemies are we ourselves and the way we read the facts. In order to develop psychologically, then, we must keep some distance from external situations which appear arbitrarily to rule our lives. We must learn to determine external situations in light of what we know of ourselves.

By nature a child is not able to understand and employ such an attitude; thus we consider infantile those who are overly responsive to external facts. The faster the reaction, the shorter the period of mediation, and thus the more our behavior is determined by a primitive, childish disposition. Maturity is characterized by taking the necessary time to evaluate a situation in order to act appropriately.

All this is the fruit of an individual effort to understand both the external world and the unconscious. That effort is what brings us into contact with the highest level of our psyche, which we call the Self. Jung has described the serious difficulties this process engenders, because "human nature has an invincible dread of becoming more conscious of itself. What nevertheless drives us to it is the self, which demands sacrifice by sacrificing itself to us."[3] In this struggle, which is not comparable to any other undertaking, "[one] suffers, so to speak, from the violence done to [one] by the self."[4]

What are the consequences of confronting fear in this way? First of all, this is not a glorification of the heroic life. As Brecht has pointed out, "Unhappy the land where heroes are needed."[5] When we become aware that external reality is always filtered through our interior world, we also understand that fear is a part of life. Like hunger, thirst or love, nature itself compels us to face our fear. Generally we do not know how to give it its proper meaning because we read it as a response to a situation that the outside world sends against us. This is a paranoid attitude that comes from denying our personal responsibility, not recognizing that we interpret events in our own way.

Fear opens a door to the unconscious. By definition what is unconscious is far from conscious awareness and so we are set in motion by unknown impulses. Any rapid reaction to external stimuli is

---

3 "Transformation Symbolism in the Mass," *Psychology and Religion,* CW 11, par. 400.

4 "A Psychological Approach to the Trinity," ibid., par. 233

5 Bertold Brecht, *Life of Galileo* (London: Methuen, 1984), p. 98.

instinctive. Reflection reduces the autonomy of the unconscious so that action takes place only after having passed the threshold of the ego. Faced with a dangerous situation, then, I come to a new understanding. The danger has become instructive.

The more fearful a situation, the more important it is to understand that the fear is nourished by our projections. In the Thematic Apperception Test there is a white card that often elicits anxiety just because it has no clear referrents. Thus it is not a question of being a hero, but of understanding that fear, though it be projected onto the outer situation, actually springs from our inner world.

Very deep personal contents emerge from a situation that causes panic. To descend into one's interior in order to grasp a meaning necessitates removing oneself ever further from the outside world. Thus, in order to recover one's own humanity and individuality, one must sacrifice external reality to the truth of the inner world.

External reality is made up of everything that surrounds us, not only people and things that are objectively frightening but also those that are beautiful and gratifying. The error we often commit is to believe that this world has a value in itself whereas it is really we who invest it with value. When we reach a point where we lose interest in externals and turn to our inner world, then we can find the meaning of the world we turned our back on.

In modern society our sense of security is so undermined that we often feel we cannot live without belonging to some kind of organization. We fear isolation. The collective is organized like a military corps that deprives us of inner security; it usurps the place of our personal mental models and presents itself as the only point of reference. In a word, we are encouraged to remain infantile, not to think independently.

We are too intimidated by these megastructures to translate them accurately and thus find it within ourselves to oppose them. Instead, we lose our most human characteristic: the ability to think. One cannot live like that. So we are obliged—and this is the perversity of the mechanism—to seek the answer to our needs outside ourselves. Thus is born the need for a leader who will take over and give us direction. Under such circumstances it is not possible to live an authentic life.

What does it mean to own a personal truth in contrast to a lie from the collective? After all, what guarantee can the individual have of the value of his or her inner life? In formulating this question we define the nucleus of the problem. Plato speaks of a type of truth that cannot be communicated,[6] referring to those moments of profound inwardness when we sense our truth and at the same time know it is ineffable. It is difficult to make oneself heard in a world that cries so much louder than we can. There is a big difference between the intuition of an inner condition and the communication of it. To put a feeling or an insight into words invariably betrays the inner experience.

It requires a good deal of courage to even try to communicate our true thoughts and feelings. In daily life we continually come into contact with people who speak in another's voice—that of the law or society or God. It is hard to speak in one's own name. When we reach an individual psychological condition that gives us the courage to expose ourselves, we experience a strange and heavy feeling of abandonment. No points of reference remain. There is neither father nor mother to bear our responsibilities. That is why we feel wounded to the core when what we express is derided.

Whenever we oppose the collective lie with our personal truth it is what we *are* that becomes the target. This triggers another painful experience we all first had in childhood: the feeling of being defenseless. I have yet to meet a single person who has never felt this way.

---

6 *The Seventh Letter* (London: Penguin, 1988).

Even those who have fulfilled their ambitions have at some time or another felt life was too much for them. We feel defenseless when we can't understand what we are doing wrong, never mind trying to figure out how to do it right. We are dismayed by the usual choices available to people. When we try to analyze them, we become aware that objects are held in higher regard than people. We feel abandoned because from that viewpoint we ourselves are negated. We must fight to see that people are given priority over the rules.

Below one of his drawings Pasolini wrote: "The world doesn't want me and doesn't know it." What could have caused this poet to say such a thing? Certainly not external events, which seemed to favor him, but rather those inner feelings which are always terribly and cruelly truthful. No destiny can evade the sound of this voice.

What should frighten us is not the feeling of being defenseless, but rather the temptation to deny this experience or label it pathological. The test that awaits us is to understand that nothing can make us secure. The only possible security we can have is to know ourselves. The world does not understand us and never will. This is clear enough in the relationship with our mother and father. As soon as we become adults with a style of our own we are abandoned. We lose our parents and it is truly a tragic experience. The big test is what happens next.

Nothing exists outside ourselves that can spare us the strain of living. The myth of the cross tells us that until the very end Jesus had to go the road of human life and, finally, speak these words: "Father, why have you forsaken me?" From a psychological viewpoint this phrase is very significant because it expresses a profoundly human condition. It is a terrible revelation, but we know it activates consciousness, even if time is required to realize it has a positive side.

It is natural that a young person should feel more intensely the need to be reassured by the love of someone else, that he or she should feel the vitality and importance of personal ambitions and desires. However, as we become adults these needs gradually become weaker and others take their place. Now it is independence we pursue. The experience of abandonment is intrinsic to this search, therefore we must not evade it.

There are many who go into analysis just when they feel lonely and abandoned. There is a risk of treating their existential situation as if it were the real problem, when what is really pathological is the way in which the person experiences solitude. It is necessary to reverse the perspective: the real question is the kind of relationship we establish with our experience of life. No one can "cure" us, because the sense of abandonment springs from an aspect of ourselves that only manifests in certain circumstances. If we do not get to know this aspect we cannot grow.

We are particularly vulnerable to the feeling of loss in love relationships. That is why people who fear being abandoned don't allow themselves to fall in love. Luckily, there is always someone who trips us up and makes us expose ourselves. To be at the mercy of someone else means to understand that nothing can protect us any more. But it also means to begin finding that personal independence that is the hallmark of maturity.

We experience abandonment not only in love but also when we put ourselves in the hands of others with power. It is a spontaneous mental reaction to believe that a powerful person can manage our lives in a positive way. This too is an illusion.

Our personal experiences derive their meaning from their specific inner context and hence can never be superimposed on, or by, those of others. It is just this personal history that is misunderstood in relationships. The uniqueness of our characteristics becomes a kind of fault and those very traits that are most our own create conflict. Though our inner truth is legitimate, it is constantly thrown into question, even when we do not in any way usurp the truth or freedom of others. The conflict this causes cannot be resolved externally but only within ourselves.

An individual life is always contradicted by the anonymous mass with its norms and sanctions. We must learn to accept this fact and bear its weight, along with the corollary that in the history of humanity the individual does not count. Underlying the great events of history there is a cruel reality: individuals are insignificant in the grand sweep of time but nevertheless endure a universe of pain.

An individual's torments only have meaning within his or her personal experience. Faced with the collective we are as naked and helpless as the day we were born. Our individual development depends on realizing that others cannot understand our experience. Sometimes the obstacles we meet tempt us to place our destiny in the hands of another. But we cannot live by proxy, we must take everything on our own shoulders. Then we know we are alone. We must allow this sensation to fill our being and live like abandoned children because only thus is our life in our own hands. From time to time a mirage will surface of some way of life that will free us from the feeling of abandonment; but a mirage is exactly what it will remain.

We can of course live solely within the collective, with the illusion of speaking a common language and of not being alone, but this deception can cost our lives. If we act according to the general rule, we are following a code that is not our own. Everyone must find his or her own tune, accepting the resulting abandonment by those who continue singing in concert. Great artists create modes of expression that are uniquely their own: they enter so deeply into their sense of life that preexisting modes no longer serve their purpose. They invent new ways of writing poetry, of painting and making music.

As individuals, our original intention is precisely to express our own nature and see it recognized by others. But innovators have no defense against persecution by the collective. When the old structures collapse, when we can no longer speak with the language we have learned nor think in the usual categories, we feel imperiled. The transition from figurative to abstract art, for instance, was a dislocation because it communicated in new terms. In such conditions the threat from outside is very grave because the new creation must hold its own against what has been long established. The old way had its beginning and its process of development, and now comes to an end. And we must do our best to grasp the symbols of the new code.

To do this involves facing our alienation and anxiety. We must return to the way we were when we were new-born. Not by chance does the motif of rebirth occur and recur in the myths of every culture, for it expresses a profound psychological truth. There is an old story about a soldier who was looking for his heart. A wise man told him, "It is at the other end of the world." The soldier went there but didn't find it. The wise man told him that in fact he had found it by going on his journey.

Psychic vitality is not inherited, nor is it to be found outside ourselves. We must create it on our own. When we live an authentic life, reality itself becomes completely different. But it isn't cheaply won, nor by cheating or craftiness. We must drink the bitter cup of confronting a world which may consider us to be an unnecessary nuisance.

Psychoanalysis too proceeds along these lines: it dismantles the codes previously used by the ego, to the point that one feels like a rudderless ship. We lose our habitual points of reference for the sake of creating new ones. In analysis we are in a kind of guided disorientation, navigating toward a new reality that has nothing to do with infantile desires to return to some timeless earthly paradise.

When we journey to "the other end of the world" to give substance to our psychic life, what awaits us is not Eden but all the contradictions of earthly life. We enlarge our capacity for understanding so that the world becomes transparent. Thus wise men retreat into solitude toward the end of their lives. But there is no sense in retiring before undertaking the journey. We meet love on the way, and whether it endures or dies, it makes life meaningful.

And death shall have no dominion.
Dead men naked they shall be one
With the man in the wind and the west moon;
When their bones are picked clean and the clean bones gone,
They shall have stars at elbow and foot;
Though they go mad they shall be sane,
Though they sink through the sea they shall rise again;
Though lovers be lost love shall not;
And death shall have no dominion.

—Dylan Thomas, "And Death Shall Have No Dominion."

Index

Books by Edward F. Edinger in this Series

SCIENCE OF THE SOUL: A Jungian Perspective
ISBN 978-1-894574-03-6. (2002) 128 pp. $25

THE PSYCHE ON STAGE: Individuation Motifs in Shakespeare and Sophocles
ISBN 978-0-919123-94-6. (2001) 96 pp. **Illustrated** $25

EGO AND SELF: The Old Testament Prophets
ISBN 978-0-919123-91-5. (2000) 160 pp. $25

THE PSYCHE IN ANTIQUITY
Book 1: Early Greek Philosophy
ISBN 978-0-919123-86-1. (1999) 128 pp. $25
Book 2: Gnosticism and Early Christianity
ISBN 978-0-919123-87-8. (1999) 160 pp. $25

THE AION LECTURES: Exploring the Self in Jung's *Aion*
ISBN 978-0-919123-72-4. (1996) 208 pp. **30 illustrations** $30

MELVILLE'S MOBY-DICK: An American Nekyia
ISBN 978-0-919123-70-0. (1995) 160 pp. $25

THE MYSTERIUM LECTURES
A Journey Through Jung's *Mysterium Coniunctionis*
ISBN 978-0-919123-66-3. (1995) 352 pp. **90 illustrations** $40

THE MYSTERY OF THE CONIUNCTIO
Alchemical Image of Individuation
ISBN 978-0-919123-67-6. (1994) 112 pp. **48 illustrations** $25

GOETHE'S FAUST: Notes for a Jungian Commentary
ISBN 978-0-919123-44-1. (1990) 112 pp. $25

THE CHRISTIAN ARCHETYPE A Jungian Commentary on the Life of Christ
ISBN 978-0-919123-27-4. (1987) 144 pp. **34 illustrations** $25

THE BIBLE AND THE PSYCHE
Individuation Symbolism in the Old Testament
ISBN 978-0-919123-23-1. (1986) 176 pp. $30

ENCOUNTER WITH THE SELF
A Jungian Commentary on William Blake's *Illustrations of the Book of Job*
ISBN 978-0-919123-21-2. (1986) 80 pp. **22 illustrations** $25

THE CREATION OF CONSCIOUSNESS: Jung's Myth for Modern Man
ISBN 978-0-919123-13-7. (1984) 128 pp. **10 illustrations** $25

Also in this Series, by Daryl Sharp

Please see next page for discounts and postage/handling.

THE SECRET RAVEN
Conflict and Transformation in the Life of Franz Kafka
ISBN 978-0-919123-00-7. (1980) 128 pp. $25

PERSONALITY TYPES: Jung's Model of Typology
ISBN 978-0-919123-30-9. (1987) 128 pp. **Diagrams** $25

THE SURVIVAL PAPERS: Anatomy of a Midlife Crisis
ISBN 978-0-919123-34-2. (1988) 160 pp. $25

DEAR GLADYS: The Survival Papers, Book 2
ISBN 978-0-919123-36-6. (1989) 144 pp. $25

JUNG LEXICON: A Primer of Terms and Concepts
ISBN 978-0-919123-48-9. (1991) 160 pp. **Diagrams** $25

GETTING TO KNOW YOU: The Inside Out of Relationship
ISBN 978-0-919123-56-4. (1992) 128 pp. $25

THE BRILLIG TRILOGY:

> **1. CHICKEN LITTLE: The Inside Story** *(A Jungian romance)*
> ISBN 978-0-919123-62-5. (1993) 128 pp. $25

> **2. WHO AM I, REALLY? Personality, Soul and Individuation**
> ISBN 978-0-919123-68-7. (1995) 144 pp. $25

> **3. LIVING JUNG: The Good and the Better**
> ISBN 978-0-919123-73-1. (1996) 128 pp. $25

JUNGIAN PSYCHOLOGY UNPLUGGED: My Life as an Elephant
ISBN 978-0-919123-81-6. (1998) 160 pp. $25

DIGESTING JUNG: Food for the Journey
ISBN 978-0-919123-96-0. (2001) 128 pp. $25

JUNG UNCORKED: Rare Vintages from the Cellar of Analytical Psychology
Four books. ISBN 978-1-894574-21-1/22-8/24-2 (2008-9) 128 pp. each. $25 each

THE SLEEPNOT TRILOGY:

> **1. NOT THE BIG SLEEP: On having fun, seriously** *(A Jungian romance)*
> ISBN 978-0-894574-13-6. (2005) 128 pp. $25

> **2. ON STAYING AWAKE: Getting Older and Bolder** *(Another Jungian romance)*
> ISBN 978-0-894574-16-7. (2006) 144 pp. $25

> **3. EYES WIDE OPEN: Late Thoughts** *(Another Jungian romance)*
> ISBN 978-0-894574-18-1.. (2007) 160 pp. $25

Studies in Jungian Psychology
by Jungian Analysts

Quality Paperbacks

Prices and payment in $US (except in Canada, $Cdn)

Jung Uncorked: Rare Vintages from the Cellar of Analytical Psychology (Four books)
Daryl Sharp (Toronto) ISBN 978-1-894574-21-1/22-8/24-2/27-3. 128 pp. $25 each

Jung and Yoga: The Psyche-Body Connection
Judith Harris (London, Ontario) ISBN 978-0-919123-95-3. 160 pp. $25

The Gambler: Romancing Lady Luck
Billye B. Currie (Jackson, MS) 978-1-894574-19-8. 128 pp. $25

Conscious Femininity: Interviews with Marion Woodman
Introduction by Marion Woodman (Toronto) ISBN 978-0-919123-59-5. 160 pp. $25

The Sacred Psyche: A Psychological Approach to the Psalms
Edward F. Edinger (Los Angeles) ISBN 978-1-894574-09-9. 160 pp. $25

Eros and Pathos: Shades of Love and Suffering
Aldo Carotenuto (Rome) ISBN 978- 0-919123-39-7. 144 pp. $25

Descent to the Goddess: A Way of Initiation for Women
Sylvia Brinton Perera (New York) ISBN 978-0-919123-05-2. 112 pp. $25

Addiction to Perfection: The Still Unravished Bride
Marion Woodman (Toronto) ISBNj 978-0-919123-11-3. Illustrated. 208 pp. $30/$35hc

The Illness That We Are: A Jungian Critique of Christianity
John P. Dourley (Ottawa) ISBN 978-0-919123-16-8. 128 pp. $25

Coming To Age: The Croning Years and Late-Life Transformation
Jane R. Prétat (Providence) ISBN 978-0-919123-63-2. 144 pp. $25

Jungian Dream Interpretation: A Handbook of Theory and Practice
James A. Hall, M.D. (Dallas) ISBN 978-0-919123-12-0. 128 pp. $25

Phallos: Sacred Image of the Masculine
Eugene Monick (Scranton) ISBN 978-0-919123-26-7. 30 illustrations. 144 pp. $25

The Sacred Prostitute: Eternal Aspect of the Feminine
Nancy Qualls-Corbett (Birmingham) ISBN 978-0-919123-31-1. Illustrated. 176 pp. $30

Longing for Paradise: Psychological Perspectives on an Archetype
Mario Jacoby (Zurich) ISBN 978-1-894574-17-4. 240 pp. $35

The Pregnant Virgin: A Process of Psychological Development
Marion Woodman (Toronto) ISBN 978-0-919123-20-5. Illustrated. 208 pp. $30pb/$35hc

Discounts: any 3-5 books, 10%; 6-9 books, 20%; 10-19, 25%; 20 or more, 40% .

Add Postage/Handling: 1-2 books, $6 surface ($10 air); 3-4 books, $8 surface ($12 air); 5-9 books, $15 surface ($20 air); 10 or more, $15 surface ($30 air)

Visa credit cards accepted. Toll-free: Tel. 1-888-927-0355; Fax 1-888=924-1814.

INNER CITY BOOKS, Box 1271, Station Q, Toronto, ON M4T 2P4, Canada

Tel. (416) 927-0355 / Fax (416) 924-1814 / booksales@innercitybooks.net